# The
# Modern
# Cottage
# Garden

# The Modern Cottage Garden

## A FRESH APPROACH TO A CLASSIC STYLE

—

**GREG LOADES**
*with photography by Neil Hepworth*

Timber Press
Portland, Oregon

Frontispiece: Romance and drama combine to create a vibrant summer scene at Churt Lea Cottage, Surrey, UK.

Published in 2020 by Timber Press, Inc.

The Haseltine Building
133 S.W. Second Avenue, Suite 450
Portland, Oregon 97204-3527
timberpress.com

Printed in China

Cover design by Stacy Wakefield Forte
Text design by Sarah Crumb

ISBN 978-1-60469-908-1
Catlog records for this book are available from the Library of Congress and the British Library.

To Malachi,
born in the year this book was written

# Contents

# What Is the Modern Cottage Garden?

It is difficult to stick to one style in the garden, isn't it?

Maybe this is because plants are alive, and as they grow, we get attached to them. So we can't let go of the plant that has survived three house moves. Or the large shrub that started life from a cutting taken from a friend's garden. Or the plant that you were sure you couldn't grow until you moved to a garden with different soil conditions to the previous one. Even if plants are not in keeping with the style of the rest of the garden or are out of proportion with the surroundings, it can be hard to let go of them. Plants are memories. Plants can make us feel proud. Plants tell stories.

And who can resist choosing new plants for the garden when they see them in flower in a nursery, even if they don't know where they will go or whether they are in keeping with what is there? Let's be honest: who

Growing good old-fashioned dahlias and asters among echinaceas, gaura, and perovskia (Russian sage) brings added boldness and charm to a display of contemporary perennials.

has a scale map of their garden, showing all the gaps, each time they find themselves looking at plants for sale? Then as we introduce unlikely plant partners to the border, we push the boundaries of traditional garden styles, whether by accident or design.

This is, in fact, a good thing. The mixing together of plants from older garden styles is creating something special indeed: a new style that combines the best of the traditional cottage garden and of the gardens of the new perennial movement. For argument's sake, let's call it the modern cottage garden.

This is a gardener's garden. Its generous style is for gardeners who can't resist plants.

It reflects, even in the small spaces where many of us garden today, the emotional ties and sentimentality of growing summer cottage garden favourites—the scented, climbing roses, bee-filled foxgloves, and dreamy hollyhocks— that speak of romance, nostalgia, and bygone days and that perhaps more than ever provide a welcome escape from the madness of our constantly changing world.

From the new perennial style it also incorporates the majestic sweeping prairie grasses and the perennials that remain as rich and colourful at the end of autumn as they were earlier, their dying stalks and bursting seedheads then offering structure and eye-catching interest in winter.

A modern cottage garden is both contemporary and classic. It celebrates diversity and shows the surprising results that can be achieved when unlikely neighbours are paired together. The modern cottage garden has been created not by deliberation or design but by people who love plants that celebrate the best of old and new.

I hope you are inspired by this book to grow plants that are new to you, to try new plant combinations and to grow plants with others where you have only grown them in isolation before, and above all to enjoy the process of experimenting with plants.

To set the mood in these pages we visit traditional and new perennial style gardens, as well as two modern cottage gardens, including my own small urban back garden. The creators of the gardens share their experience and offer up interesting thoughts for the keen gardener.

Roses (here, 'Roald
Dahl') are a main-
stay of the classic
cottage garden and
are often grown in
isolation, but they
can blend beauti-
fully with different
plants in a border.

For many of us, gardening means fitting more and more into smaller
spaces: grow plants from traditional cottage gardens and the new perennial style next to each other in pots and there are even more possibilities,
as plants that have different needs can be shown off side by side. A garden
primarily made up of plants in pots will have a big impact in small spaces.

Being bold at planting new plants together can make your garden and
your gardening life more exciting than it's ever been. There's nothing to
lose. The worst that can happen if a plant fails is that you have the opportunity to replace it with something else. See the many suggestions in
this book, including a directory of fifty essential plants for the modern
cottage garden.

The range of available plant varieties has only increased as the new
perennial style has brought attention to many late-summer-flowering
perennials. Also continuing to tug at our heartstrings are memories of the
romantic roses that grew over the front door of our grandparents' house

or the heavenly mix of herbaceous cottage garden perennials that make English country gardens a place of pilgrimage for serious garden visitors.

Growing prairie plants and classic cottage garden varieties together may seem like two completely different approaches to gardening, but in the same way that your palate changes as you embrace food from around the world, so tastes in plants can broaden as gardeners become more adventurous. Your options don't have to be either-or. You can have both approaches in the same garden and even in the same terracotta pot or hanging basket.

Put these two styles together and what do you have? A new but classic style of garden. Think Bing Crosby and David Bowie singing "Little Drummer Boy" together. The surprising pairing of the new guard and the old, the new perennial garden and the cottage garden, can make something beautiful. (I also offer guidance for caring for your plants through the seasons and for the long term.)

Peace on earth, can it be? In our gardens, yes.

Red heleniums and the yellow daisy flowers of rudbeckias are star plants of the new perennial garden and blend well with cottage garden favourites pot marigold and white Shasta daisies.

# Roots

We begin this journey with a look at two foundational gardening styles that underpin our sensibilities today: the romantic cottage garden revival of the nineteenth and early twentieth centuries and the new perennial style—which has its own kind of romance—at the turn of the millennium.  >

Billowing clouds of blossoms from rose 'Ballerina' are a hallmark of the traditional cottage garden, seen here at Newby Hall in Yorkshire, UK.

Traditional cottage gardens were packed with flowers that self-seeded into informal layouts in summer primarily. But fast forward into the twenty-first century and the desire for plants that work hard to add interest throughout the year came to the fore as gardening space and spare time for gardening decreased.

By the turn of the millennium, the new perennial garden was the new style, with swathes of grasses and perennials planted together. In garden shows you may have noticed a fashion for perennials with evergreen and deciduous grasses featured at the expense of the sacred cows of roses, foxgloves, and flowering shrubs, which were suddenly deemed unfashionable.

Yet romance will never die and that's where the new modern cottage garden comes in.

# The Traditional Cottage Garden

What do I mean by "cottage garden" and what do gardeners mean when they say they want elements of the cottage garden in their outdoor space?

This style emphasizes a palette of soft, pastel colours: an abundance of pink and purple and frothy white blossom from crab apples, rambling roses, airy cosmos, and heavenly scented tobacco plants. Borders are crammed with flowering plants—usually flanked by lawn—with the peak season being that moment when spring and summer collide, with the first roses, foxgloves, and delphiniums all flowering together. Sprawling honeysuckles and clematis cover walls and boundaries, frothy *Alchemilla mollis* lines border edges, and there is an emphasis on plants being allowed to gently go off course to naturally colonize areas. In this higgledy-piggledy scene of well-organized chaos, self-seeding is encouraged, with drifts of random foxgloves and hollyhocks popping up in summer and flowering herbs nestling beneath.

It is on the whole a wildlife-friendly garden, with simple single flowers loved by pollinating insects, and a rich tapestry of jumbled up planting eliminating the need for plants to be manipulated or for weeds to be controlled with herbicides.

It is a style of garden that resonates with the reclaimed, the aged, and the old-fashioned. Picture the gently crumbling old brick wall, the rickety garden

gate, the weathered wooden arches bedecked in a wispy honeysuckle that threatens to take the structure down every year, making a more beautiful feature as it takes over more ground. Think shabby chic with plants.

The great advantage of the cottage garden style of planting is that in summer the amount of maintenance required is low. Because the style is informal and plants are encouraged to mingle together in a tight space, there is no need for endless preening and staking of plants to make the garden look more ordered.

However, the truth about cottage gardens is that their apparent randomness is really only achieved with skillful editing and planning of which plants are allowed to go where. In fact, there is a lot of work to be done behind the scenes in early spring in order to prevent total messiness. If plants are allowed to self-seed without control and vigorous perennials not divided regularly to restrict their spread, then a handful of plants can dominate the garden, which will lose its diversity of colour and form.

The cottage garden's star performers also have a habit of peaking in early summer and then disappearing or never quite hitting the heights of flowering performance and health later in the year. Herbs, old roses, foxgloves, and lady's mantle (*Alchemilla*) delight and charm the gardener as spring merges into summer, but just six weeks later their flowers are distant memories and they can leave big colour gaps in the garden.

## A BRIEF HISTORY

If you are sitting comfortably, here's a brief history of the cottage garden to set the scene. Originally cottage gardens in Britain were small but productive spaces around a cottage where herbs, vegetables, flowers, and livestock all lived in (supposed) harmony. The cottages would be home for farm workers who had to make their limited space as productive as possible to feed their household.

It was in the Victorian era that two famous gardeners, Gertrude Jekyll and William Robinson, started planting crammed, flower-packed gardens, with informal layouts, influenced by the original cottage gardens. This reinterpretation became popular and over time took with it the cottage

The flower garden at Gravetye Manor contains a wonderful array of herbs, perennials, and annuals flowering together to create a wild-looking cottage garden.

garden label. So now the name referred more to that romantic vision of spires of foxgloves, rambling roses, herbs, and self-seeding annual plants that gardeners are still influenced by today, and lost the productive elements that were its original purpose (and often, the cottage as well).

In 1885 William Robinson started creating a garden at Gravetye Manor in Sussex, UK, with the emphasis on creating a colourful garden that worked with nature. Robinsons' philosophy was that gardens shouldn't strictly follow a layout and should develop naturally, with the emphasis on plants that would return year on year, rather than annual bedding plants that need replacing and replanting each year. Robinson also championed the idea of mixed borders, where shrubs, hardy, and half-hardy perennials would grow together. His garden at Gravetye was grand, a far cry from the small strips of garden around humble cottage dwellings, but his approach still forms the framework for what many gardeners consider a cottage garden to be today.

As Robinson and Jekyll put their own modernized stamp on the cottage garden idea, so the style changed further through the generations. In the late 1930s Margery Fish began to create her extraordinary garden at East Lambrook Manor Gardens in Somerset, UK. Fish used a high proportion of perennials in the garden and inventively planted it with ornamentals that would look good all year round, with a much longer flowering period.

In essence, the cottage garden continues to change through the generations. Perhaps what a lot of gardeners aim to achieve when they think of creating a cottage garden is an area of planting that is heavily influenced by the cottage garden style found in many of the great British gardens: the herbaceous border.

William Robinson's emphasis was on creating a full and colourful garden without using bedding plants, as seen in the flower garden at Gravetye Manor in early autumn.

## THE HERBACEOUS BORDER

The herbaceous border could be considered the high-maintenance, well-to-do cousin (do you have one of those in your family?) of the cottage garden. Originally the preserve of large country-house landscapes, it would be used to line walls and hedges around the margins of a large garden, hence the term *border*. The *herbaceous* part of the name refers to the

garden being made up exclusively of perennial plants that die down each winter before starting into growth again the following spring.

Although often more formal in layout, the herbaceous border bears many hallmarks of the cottage garden: it is packed with flowers, and plants are crammed together to make the most of the space on offer.

Traditionally tall plants would be planted at the back of the herbaceous border, with their height sloping down to ground-covering plants such as alchemillas and hardy geraniums that clothed the edge of the border. When made up exclusively of perennial plants, these areas of the garden are extremely labour-intensive. Because the plants start growing from scratch each year, growth is fragile and most plants need staking

from early spring onwards. The border is bare during winter and for a lot of spring, making weeding an essential task for the impatient gardener waiting for the desirable perennials to cover the bare ground.

The overall effect of the herbaceous border is of a formal showpiece that reaches its peak of flowering in midsummer. While this undoubtedly offers a tremendous garden spectacle, the herbaceous border is something of a luxury for the gardener lacking space. The season of interest is relatively short, and the hours of staking, weeding, cutting back, and watering only give rewards in summer and autumn. In winter the border is a barren landscape, devoid of structure, colour, and life.

**Above left:** Summer-flowering perennials add colour around a robust structure of evergreens at East Lambrook Manor Gardens in Somerset, UK.

**Above:** The Silver Garden at East Lambrook Manor Gardens is packed with cottage garden classics and Mediterranean shrubs.

**Above right:** The cottage garden style of planting is packed, informal, colourful, and evocative of times past.

**Overleaf:** The cottage garden style reaches its peak at the beginning of summer and features free-flowering perennials packed together, often with flowers in pastel shades, as shown here at Newby Hall, UK.

The exclusive use of perennials in an area of the garden enjoyed a renaissance in the second half of the twentieth century, thanks in large part to UK plantsman Alan Bloom. He pioneered the idea of growing perennials in beds rather than borders. These would be areas of bare earth cut into the lawn in flowing shapes—kidney-shaped or circular—and planted with perennials that could be viewed from all sides, with no top and bottom. Although still labour intensive, perennial beds were smaller and less formal than herbaceous borders.

An herbaceous border
in full bloom in high
summer at Newby Hall
in Yorkshire, UK.

# A Traditional Herbaceous Border that Pays Homage to the Cottage Garden

## Newby Hall, Yorkshire, UK

The gardens of the stately home at Newby Hall in North Yorkshire in the north of England are a tremendous example of the traditional herbaceous border inspired by the cottage garden style, with many popular and effective cottage garden perennials shown off, reaching a peak of colour in summer.

The borders have been planted at Newby Hall since the 1920s, but in former head gardener Mark Jackson's words, the planting options available to a gardener making a traditional border have increased dramatically with access to a far greater range of perennial plants. He says that herbaceous plants used to be associated with having a lull between high and late summer, but that has fundamentally changed: "Many of the perennials in the border, such as asters, echinacea, and eutrochium, have impact from the start of summer until well into autumn. Eliminating the lull brings the herbaceous border back into the limelight again."

The dreamy spires of delphinium flowers—a trademark of the cottage garden—have been a constant in the borders throughout the years so that despite a major replanting, Mark kept delphiniums as a key plant because of their timeless appeal: "They are quite a difficult plant to grow because they are difficult to stake, but when they do their thing, it is quite a feature."

Mark also grew annuals in the border—another historical mainstay of the traditional cottage garden—but he is selective, using cleomes and cosmos as filler plants and dahlias to hold the design together at the end of summer.

The borders are cut down in the second half of winter, so that the chance to enjoy the skeletal features of the taller perennials is not completely jettisoned by the regime of cutting back: "A shaft of light on an ageing stem of datisca while the sun is setting can look special."

The borders at Newby are 4m (13ft) wide, so backbone plants at the rear of the border have to be managed to avoid forming clumps that encroach too far into the border. "The planting is moving away from the planed-off angle with plants rising in height from the front of the border to the back, which is very traditional," Mark says.

Instead he spaced plants so that they disappear from one angle but can be seen from another. He also champions the use of see-through plants that carry thin, loose stems, *Verbena bonariensis* being a classic example. "The height of the border is varied throughout. As I walk along the border I am always looking for undulations in the planting."

Mark is aware that if he is not careful, plants can look artificially placed in a traditional border, especially at the front, where if all the plants are small, they don't look as if they are linked to the rest of the border.

The plants in the borders are encouraged to have an openness to them, rather than being staked for their entire height. "We liked the plants to have a little bit of 'lean' to them," he noted. However, Mark sees the reputation of herbaceous plants as being hard work to look after as not completely true. "Yes, you can't just stick them in and walk away from them, but the good thing about perennials is that it is easy to sort the plants out if something goes wrong. You can move them around if they are in the wrong place, and remove parts of the plant if necessary."

Mark divided a lot of herbaceous plants in autumn when the soil was still warm and the plant still had top growth on it. This made it easier to see what he had than if he waited until early spring. "It also means that the memories of summer are still in your mind when you are deciding where to move new divisions of the plant."

The time to divide is not easy to put a finger on, according to Mark. "Observe your plants and see what issues start to happen," he said. "If the plant is not producing as many flowers as it was before, or the plant has become hollow, with all the growth on the outside, then it is telling you that it needs to be divided."

The whole border used to be netted, but now only the back 3m (10ft) has mesh draped over stakes to cover every plant. The staking is carried out at the last possible moment to allow time to enjoy the diversity of colours and daily changing display of new growth sprouting through the soil surface. The delay also allows weeding to be easily done beforehand.

The borders at Newby Hall are not traditionally tiered with a top and a bottom (tall plants at the back and shorter plants up front), but instead plants can be viewed through each other because of their different growth habits—a trick that can be used when combining traditional and contemporary garden styles.

Mark dispensed with formal bedding plants when the border was revamped. Formal bedding plants are still a popular addition to some historic house gardens in the UK, especially if the gardener has a mandate to preserve the heritage of the planting so that it reflects previous generations. The wide use of summer-flowering annuals that would be killed by frost in winter and then replanted again at the end of the following spring was a way of showing bright colours on a grand scale, but the plants such as zonal pelargoniums, African marigolds, and dwarf salvias do not blend well with flowering perennials in a border.

In his planting decisions Mark chose to reinforce the "three I's":

**Identity** Visitors expected a traditional herbaceous border at Newby Hall so that is what they would get.

**Individuality** The borders would be very definitely Newby's and not a replica of another.

**Integrity** The border would work as a whole and would not be split into different sections.

# The New Perennial Garden

Think of a garden that is largely made of flowering perennials, grasses, and sedges, with fountains of seedheads providing much of the height and structure. In among the moving sea of wispy foliage are tough perennial plants such as echinaceas, salvia, scabious, and perennial rudbeckias peppering the late summer greens and browns with shots of colour that will be allowed to fade to an exquisite monochrome, as the whole garden is kept intact for winter.

The new perennial garden is one that flows, with no straight lines, instead sinuous paths of planting held together with pockets of colourful perennials.

Think waves of planting through large beds or borders, with the movement of wispy grasses making the garden atmospheric on a blustery day, even on a stormy day in winter when being outside in the garden is at the bottom of even a keen gardener's to-do list. Strong winds enhance and animate the garden rather than potentially destroying precious soft growth on delicate plants.

This style emphasizes structure, with perennial seedheads and dormant wands of foliage having as much impact as the most colourful of summer flowers. A strong backbone of plants stays intact in the garden until the end of winter, when last year's growth finally starts to flatten and go soggy.

Typical plants of the new perennial style include echinacea, sedum, and stipa (nassella), seen here in the gardens at Dove Cottage Nursery in Halifax, UK.

The new perennial garden is naturalistic, meaning that it is supposed to look natural, as if the plants that are grown together are growing in the wild. This is an illusion rather than a reality in some cases, with the plants originating from eclectic backgrounds, but when executed well, the approach creates some truly breathtaking landscapes that are the polar opposite to formal, structured, herbaceous borders.

The style can also be genuinely naturalistic. Among its most famous proponents is Dutch plantsman and designer Piet Oudolf, who has been labeled the godfather of the new perennial movement, which became the title for this style of garden creation. In his designs Oudolf champions the use of communities of plants—plants that would grow together naturally in the same habitat.

The new perennial garden is to be enjoyed as if watching an old film being restored to colour in reverse. The abundant light show comes first, before the subtle characters and the storyline become prominent when the colour is drained from the narrative. Roses and annual plants are nowhere to be seen, and loud yellow and bright blue flowers are used sparingly.

In fact, Oudolf's approach is to concentrate more on the different shapes, structures, and textures that can be seen in the garden than on the colour of the flowers, and when he came to prominence at the turn of the century this thinking was—and largely still is—revolutionary. Gardeners are in equal parts attracted, offended, and delighted by colours, which are most often the primary consideration when we choose a plant to add to our gardens. It's only natural, in the same way that if we meet up with a friend we will comment on the colour of their clothing, either stating that we like it or that it is not to our taste.

Self-seeding, as with eryngiums, helps create the feeling of a natural display, as seen in the gardens at Dove Cottage Nursery in Halifax, UK.

But Oudolf's style is all about foresight, not just about what colours the plant will bring to the garden when in full flower, but what it has to contribute to the garden in terms of form and structure when summer is but a memory. By prioritizing structure, form, shape, and texture he creates gardens and planting combinations that are effective for a long time, from the end of spring to the end of winter. They are gardens that would still look beautiful in black and white.

The beauty of Oudolf's philosophy is that it can open the mind of even the most old-fashioned gardener and enhance the beauty of the planting combinations they choose. When we consider what a plant will look like as it ages and choose accordingly, the garden can look attractive for longer without such sporadic highs and lows of interest.

This approach to creating a garden in some ways reduces the maintenance involved. The whole garden can simply be cut back unceremoniously—by strimmer and lawnmower at the Oudolf-designed Millennium Garden at Pensthorpe Natural Park—at the end of winter in one fell swoop. There is no intricate pruning of shrubs or roses to be done, and no replacement of annuals. Plants are largely left to self-seed, with the removal only of those that are muscling in too much on the territory of others.

## AND YET: BEYOND THE NEW PERENNIAL GARDEN

The new perennial style is unquestionably a thing of beauty, showing perennial plants from flowering through to the end of winter. But if grasses are allowed to take over, then the garden can become a monoculture with a short season of interest, only starting to look its finest towards the end of summer.

If you have the luxury of lots of space to recreate large swathes of grasses mixed with late-blooming perennials, then the results won't lack for diversity. A large, west-facing border of prairie plants would exhaust the batteries of many a smart-phone in late summer, providing the perfect decoration for photographing a sunset. Yet the famous garden

styles can feel too regular, where one group of plants is central (think of a Japanese garden full of colourful maples, cherries, and pines).

Many gardeners are drawn beyond such limitations. Those of us who love growing all kinds of plants find it difficult to be constrained to the select few species of a single planting style. In smaller spaces especially (and for every gardener who complains about having too much space I'll show you twenty who would give their right arm for a few extra square yards) a more eclectic planting scheme can have more impact and over a longer period of the year too.

Mix up a yearning for plants from our past with an open mind to try growing new plants—the ability to find space for just one more plant is

always good too—and you will create a garden that is varied, colourful, fragrant, stylish, and transferrable to a space of any size or shape, or even simply to containers. Grow late-flowering perennials, sedges, and grasses alongside classic cottage garden plants and your modern cottage garden can look good all year round, especially if you consider the structure that these plants can bring to the garden once summer has gone.

# Piet Oudolf's Perennial Meadow at Scampston Walled Garden

Yorkshire, UK

At the Perennial Meadow at Scampston Walled Garden in Yorkshire in autumn, the prominent structure of seedheads starts to subtly define the landscape.

The Perennial Meadow at Scampston Walled Garden in Yorkshire, UK, was designed by Piet Oudolf in 1999 and bears all the hallmarks of the new perennial style of gardening that he made famous across the world. The garden is laid out in a modern twist on a formal design, with four symmetrical rectangular flowerbeds, each with a corner cut off to create a central seating area. Yet the traditional framework is hidden among a tapestry of perennials and grasses that are artfully woven together to complement each other right through the growing season.

In the perennial meadow Oudolf focussed on plants that would work well together. As he told me, "I used lots of plants of similar heights together so that you can sit in the garden but not feel locked up, and then when you stand you can see out to the rest of the garden."

Pinks and purples are the most common colours in this part of the garden in summer, with drifts of the purple thistle-like flowers of *Cirsium rivulare* 'Atro-purpureum' and *Echinacea pallida*, combining with the purple-blue stems of *Perovskia* 'Blue Spire'. Oudolf used a restricted colour palette because some colours are known to dominate in the garden. Pinks and purples are the easiest colours on the eye, and they tend to not be as distracting as bolder colours such as yellow, as he says:

*Yellow is a very dominant colour in the garden because it leads your eye towards it. I like yellow but I don't use it too much, especially in summer. It is a main colour in the garden in spring and it is part of the full experience of fall when it shows with shades of brown on old foliage, but in summer I only use it a little.*

The tightly woven planting takes on a new dimension by autumn, with the colour palette still visible in the hot pink flowers of *Sedum* 'Matrona', but it is blended with shades of brown and maroon as seedheads age and grasses glow in the low sunlight.

"My gardens are based on durability and a seasonality so that plants provide a long season of interest," he said. "It is the opposite of the traditional garden border, which is more focussed on flowers and blooming times and when the flowering is over it's all done."

Leaving the garden intact to be framed by frost avoids the emptiness found in so many gardens in winter and eliminates the need for lots of maintenance in

autumn and winter as well as reducing the need for additional planting. Oudolf explained:

*At the time I designed Scampston, gardens weren't about plants growing together with others as part of a community. Most gardens involved a lot of maintenance because they relied partly on annual or biennial plants, which require constant replanting. Plants were added as individuals, and the season of interest in the garden could be very short-lived.*

Twenty years on from designing Scampston, Piet told me that his style hasn't really changed, but that he now concentrates on low-maintenance communities of plants in a garden:

*Plants are grown for more than just the flowers—they have to have other qualities through the year. My thinking that I want to make a garden more than just about the flowers has become stronger over time. Seedheads in particular are very valuable for wildlife and also for the eyes because of the visual appeal they add to the garden in winter. I think that now gardeners are starting to accept more than ever that gardens can look appealing as they start to die off in autumn and winter.*

Grasses glisten in the sunlight among the sea of seedheads that have been deliberately left intact as the garden becomes a masterpiece of architecture until the end of winter.

# How to Create a Modern Cottage Garden

What a time to be a gardener! Never in human history has there been such an incredible choice of plants readily available to anybody wanting to plant a garden. >

The wide diversity of plants available to gardeners today allows for exciting experimentation, as seen at the garden at 39 Foster Road, Cambridgeshire, UK. This is a private garden but it opens to the public each year as part of the National Garden Scheme.

Like a kid in a sweet shop trying to get familiar with the full range of jelly bean flavours, so we are spoiled for choice as we experiment with growing different plants. And if we can be as curious and inquisitive as a child choosing candy when we consider different plants to grow in our gardens, then the possibilities are exciting and the results rewarding (and plants won't rot your teeth either).

Spontaneity is a hallmark of the modern cottage garden. It is a style that has evolved as gardeners try to grow more exotic and eclectic plants. Like adding "fusion" to your home cooking after going on vacation abroad or adding an avocado to a bacon and egg breakfast, you'll discover that some things just work together well that you never thought would.

Nostalgia affects the way we garden because plants are evocative things. Their scents help us relive days gone by; their flowers serve as marker points in the year, reminding us of springs and summers of long ago but that feel like yes-terday. Our urge to grow many of the cottage garden plants that were readily available to our parents or grandparents (the poppies, rambling roses, clematis, and foxgloves, to name but a few) is to relive times and loved ones past.

The urge of the keen gardener to go outside in the pouring rain and potter—that yearning to sow some seeds on the windowsill in the depths of winter—may be part instinct but is more likely also a result of the past, of spending time with that older relative, that aunt, uncle, parent, or grandparent

The urge to go out and garden often comes from being inspired by somebody from the previous generation.

who grew plants and couldn't wait to share the joy and therapy of growing plants with the next generations: you and me.

Taking the best bits from our own gardening stories and combining them with the traditional cottage and new perennial styles can give us a garden that is personally meaningful and a pleasure to grow. So let's get started.

# Planting a Gardener's Garden

A gardener's garden is never finished. It evolves as we make new discoveries and get inspired by visiting other gardens and seeing plants that we have never grown before.

In fact, the original cottage garden was not really a designed garden at all but rather one of necessity, and of letting plants have the freedom to spread. Elements of order and design crept in with the advent of the herbaceous border, and today our modern cottage garden borrows from both these earlier approaches. It is not an overly designed space; instead it grows organically. Yet there are also some design and planting principles that will help you succeed whether you are laying out a garden from scratch or incorporating a new approach into your existing space.

**Design for spontaneity** Create a garden of flowing shapes from the way that plants are arranged and paths are laid out, rather than of stuffy, straight lines.

Then plant out the largest, structural plants first. Evergreen shrubs or perennials and small trees will give you a solid framework to fill in with your diverse and exciting, colourful, impulse buys and nostalgic flowers. It's like baking a cake and then going crazy with the icing and decorations.

Most gardeners find it difficult *not* to buy plants to add to their garden in spring.

**Be curious about plants** New additions to the garden are often based on impulse. Plants are of the moment in a way that inanimate objects are not. Their flowers, leaves, and scents project the joy of a season, a living moment that speaks of hope in spring, abundance in summer, wistful reflection in autumn, and the sheer relief of seeing something colourful to grab and plant in the garden in winter. That's why it's so hard for plantaholics to stop buying plants when they visit nurseries and see them growing. The idea that buying plants for the garden in a piecemeal way is in some way wrong is absurd to anyone who is captivated by plants.

**Embrace change in the garden** As long as we look at gardens and plants to allow ourselves to encounter new ones, our gardens will keep changing as our obsession with plants leads inevitably to a garden that mixes styles, one that is full of planting that is fresh, colourful, and artistic—a garden that gives a nostalgic nod to the past but with a modern twist.

**Garden in small spaces** Making the most of the diversity of plants on offer helps overcome the frustration of lack of growing space. In fact, having to plant within a concentrated area makes it easier to keep the

Mixing grasses with flowering perennials such as achilleas that age well in winter is a good way to extend the season of interest in a garden (seen here at Dove Cottage Nursery, Halifax, UK) especially in small spaces, to make the garden look good for longer.

garden looking focused and thematic. Yes, you might not have room for sweeping glades of shimmering grasses, but you can offer a taste of all the facets that make the new perennial style and the traditional cottage garden such desirable styles to emulate.

Think of a small garden as a restaurant that serves up only small amounts of food but offers the finest combinations of flavours rather than "piling it high and selling it cheap." This is no bad thing. After all, these are often the most exciting and surprising places to eat.

**Plan for all seasons in the garden** A great way to make the most of small spaces in the garden—and especially in the modern cottage garden—is to grow plants that complement each other, with each offering more than one season of interest.

Growing a wider diversity of plants that flower at different times will change your garden from a space that is enjoyed for a month or two as it peaks and quickly fades, to a space that looks good throughout the seasons.

The most prominent plants in the traditional cottage garden tend to have one thing in common: they flower in summer and can start to lose colour and also foliage lustre well before the arrival of autumn. The blending of this style with the new perennial style automatically creates a planting scheme that has a steady level of interest for a much longer period.

A strength of the new perennial planting style and surely a reason for its popularity is that it peaks much later in the year than a traditional

**Opposite:** The mix of ageing grasses and bold, late-flowering perennials such as *Sedum* 'Matrona' is as spectacular as any scene in summer.

cottage garden's planting scheme. Many prairie plants are at their peak of flowering late in the growing season and are accompanied by the brilliant, burnished shades of a host of perennial grasses. Autumn becomes a celebration of all sorts of plants and not just the leaf colours on trees. Many of the perennials in the style such as *Helenium* 'Moerheim Beauty', *Rudbeckia fulgida*, and *Salvia nemorosa*, start flowering in mid to late summer and keep showing vibrant colour well into autumn.

The season of interest is stretched further by the fusion of the colourful foliage and flowers of grasses such as golden *Calamagrostis ×acutiflora* 'Karl Foerster', straw-coloured tassels of *Deschampsia cespitosa* complementing the subdued faded hues of the last flowers of echinaceas and the late domed flowerheads of purple-pink *Sedum* 'Matrona' which edge borders with a final burst of bright colour.

To borrow the early summer peak of the traditional cottage garden and add it to the late season peak of the new perennial garden means you have a garden that is abundant and full for half of the year. And all this before the prairie plants perform their final trick of the year, when their stark but prominent structures remain standing in winter, to take on an ethereal presence as the hoar frost frames the detail in their seedheads and ageing leaves.

The garden becomes like a cherished photograph of an aged loved one. There is joy in seeing the detail of an instantly recognizable face and with it wistful memories of the exuberance and energy of past youth. As with loved ones it is the same with appreciating the garden throughout the year. It has survived ups and downs, storms and sunshine and looks different from before but you love it as much as at any other time.

**Consider basic conditions** Part of the joy of gardening is experimenting and learning about plants and to what extent they are adaptable. If a plant is a sun-lover, it won't flower as well if planted in shade. Soil types will also play a part. If a plant such as a shrub rose favours heavy clay soil, then it might not grow as strongly on a soil that is light and sandy. Or if a plant needs acid soil, then growing it in a limey soil will be a futile exercise.

If plants aren't growing in their ideal conditions, however, they can still grow well, so don't be afraid to experiment. And if you really don't have the conditions for a particular plant that you want (full shade when you need full sun, for example), then container growing is always an option.

**Make use of containers** The most obvious place to merge styles is in flower beds and borders, but the modern cottage garden style also lends itself to fresh and colourful recipes for patio containers and even hanging baskets. A simple container planted with three plants that produce eye-catching foliage, flowers, stems, and berries can look interesting and colourful all through the growing season. Patio containers often feature one plant in isolation but this is a missed opportunity in many cases, especially in small gardens, unless you are trying to make a formal garden where every plant has its place.

Hanging baskets are well due our attention after years of these splendid garden features simply being associated with only a narrow group of plants. There is so much more potential in hanging baskets than simply growing trailing fuchsias and petunias, even though these plants have their merits. Hanging baskets are also invaluable at keeping slugs at bay (despite their persistence they haven't learned how to climb ladders yet).

**Below:** Adding horticultural grit to the soil and mixing it in well will instantly improve the drainage of your garden soil and make it possible to grow a wider range of plants.

**Below right:** Container growing allows you to grow plants in the garden that may not be suited to the type of soil, and there is the added bonus of being able to pair them with plants that like different conditions, growing in nearby containers.

**Allow plants to self sow, to a point** In the traditional cottage garden, plants are allowed to set seed, resulting in a lively randomness that speaks of abundance and of nature being accommodated, if not quite granted free rein. Some stray seedlings will be pulled out, but unlike a formal garden, the modern cottage garden is not a place where every plant has its allotted spot.

Allowing plants to self-seed is a more natural and cost-effective way of introducing swathes of plants into a garden than by planting potted plants, but there is a danger. If all flowers are allowed to spread, the bullies win out over the slow-developers. *Verbena bonariensis*, *Erigeron karvinskianus*, and aquilegias can start to steal more than their fair share of the garden, and in a small space they are as exasperating as a passenger on a jam-packed train who insists on spreading out all their luggage and personal effects.

Allowing greedy self-seeders to run riot can leave you with an imbalanced garden that looks in one way abundant but in another way one-dimensional, and plants can lose their impact in the garden. One classic culprit of this is *Alchemilla mollis*. Used sparingly or as a deliberately planted edging plant in a formal garden, it can look wonderful—if only for a short period in high summer. But if it sets seed and becomes a mass planting, it dominates the garden and its impact is gone.

To desire a garden that looks natural is one thing, but remember that a rule of nature is survival of the fittest and self-seeding plants taking over is a manifestation of this mantra. If plants are allowed to take over a large percentage of the garden, then too few plants end up doing too much of the work, and this is always noticeable.

If you want to enjoy the beauty of sparkling frosted seedheads in the garden in winter with all its sporadic splendour, chopping the plants down to stop them seeding is not an option. Instead, wait until seedlings appear in the following spring and pull out those that you don't want. It may feel like sacrilege, but if a weed is a plant growing in the wrong place, then even seedlings of your favourite flowers fall into this category if they are threatening to spoil the balance of the garden. You can always put young seedlings into pots of equal parts multipurpose compost and

Allowing plants such as orange pot marigolds to set seed can create an informal style typical of the traditional cottage garden.

garden soil, grow them on in a shady corner, and give them away to neighbours once they are well rooted.

**Set the tone with bold boundaries** Garden boundaries often dictate the style of garden that is made within them. If you have a garden with smooth, rendered walls, then an old-fashioned cottage garden will not look as good as if it was backed by an old, slightly weathered brick wall. However, the modern cottage garden will work well with any background in the garden, be it shiny walls, brand new timber, crumbling walls, or even gabions or wire cages filled with rocks.

Work with what you have. Old brick walls are made for having old-fashioned climbers such as *Lonicera periclymenum*, sweet peas, and *Clematis montana* scrambling over them, while rusty metal boundaries are the perfect backdrop for showing off the form of tall grasses such as *Panicum virgatum* and tall perennials such as *Verbena bonariensis*.

A boundary that filters light will greatly enhance the atmosphere and mix of colours in a modern cottage garden border. Flowers with translucent petals such as echinaceas and heleniums will positively glow in the evening sun, as will grasses with broad leaves such as *Hakonechloa macra* 'Aureola' and 'Nicolas' with its orangey red foliage, and the soft flowerheads of *Stipa tenuissima* and *Pennisetum villosum*.

A wide-open border with no obvious physical backdrop will make maximum use of the sun, but leggy perennials may need staking to keep them upright. If staking seems laborious and/or expensive, then growing shorter varieties is a low-maintenance option.

Rusted metal is the perfect backdrop for showing off purple flowers such as *Verbena bonariensis*, and it also complements the muted shades of flowering grasses.

Jenny Bowden's garden contains
a blend of cottage garden flowers,
late-flowering perennials, sun-
loving Mediterranean plants, and
even a banana, although it needs
frost protection.

# A Modern Cottage Garden at Churt Lea Cottage

## Surrey, UK

Jenny Bowden's hillside garden is a wonderful example of the versatility and endless possibilities of the modern cottage garden.

Self-seeding plants add a looseness and a flow to the garden, which evokes memories of the classic cottage garden style, but with new perennial plants such as the dripping wands of the golden oat grass *Stipa gigantea* and the architectural purple thistle *Cynara cardunculus*, the old and new styles blend together perfectly.

Although pale pink is her "ultimate dislike" in the garden, Jenny loves colour, with warm oranges, purples, and blues providing combinations that are more reminiscent of the new perennial movement palette. But there is a real diversity in the plants used around the garden. "I was a student at RHS Wisley in the 1990s when the new perennial movement was quite new and it definitely appealed to me," says Jenny.

A mixture of lawn and curvy brick paths provides a further nod to the cottage garden, while California poppies, catmint, and perennial salvias mix old-fashioned charm with new perennial structure and colour. Jenny pondered the question of whether to include a lawn for a while, but for contrast and to be easy on the eye, it was used to enhance the view down the plot towards the pond at the end of the garden.

The garden at Churt Lea Cottage is sited on a south-facing hillside. In the spirit of true collaboration, Jenny's husband, Nigel, carried out all the clearing and leveling and created a blank canvas with a tractor and a digger. It is a largely open garden where most of the plants are exposed to full sun although some areas are in partial shade.

**Top left:** Both the romance of the cottage garden and the drama of the new perennial garden are allowed to sit side-by-side in opposite borders to create a diverse and vibrant summer scene.

**Left:** The garden is laid out with a mixture of curved and straight paths, a patio area, and a lawn separating the areas of planting.

This may sound idyllic, but the soil makes it a potentially challenging space in which to create a beautiful garden. The soil is, in Jenny's words, "like dust": "When you dig into it, the wind blows it away!" she explains. The garden is also in a relatively warm and dry part of the UK.

Although she would like the plantings to be resplendent in some of the well-known cottage garden staples such as phlox and roses, the soil simply isn't suitable. Instead, Jenny has cleverly picked out some elements of the cottage garden that can work in the space.

California poppies (*Eschscholzia californica*; above left), pot marigolds (*Calendula officinalis*; right), and erigerons (*Erigeron karvinskianus*; above right) are effective self-seeders and add a colorful, informal style to the border edges.

For example, drifts of self-seeding plants proved invaluable in providing flowers and fullness in the garden's early years when shrubs and perennials were taking their time to fill out and make the garden feel mature.

Jenny's vision wasn't to create a traditional cottage garden, though, but something more eclectic that would work in the challenging conditions and that fitted her "rules" for the garden. Jenny had clear ideas about the plants that she wanted. They had to be low-maintenance and able to survive and look good without constant watering: "The garden is watered two or three times each

**Opposite, top:**
The bright orange and yellow shades in the flowers of *Alstroemeria* Indian Summer blend immaculately with the fresh foliage of *Nandina domestica*, which shows subtle changes of red and bronze.

**Opposite, bottom:**
The dark purple leaves of *Persicaria microcephala* 'Red Dragon' (bottom left) make a fine foil for the greyish purple spikes of lavender and the hot pink flowers of *Lychnis coronaria*. Together these plants provide a deep contrast with the oranges, yellows, and lime greens in the opposite border.

**Right:** The beautiful fountain of golden flowers from new perennial favourite *Stipa gigantea* provide a spectacular backdrop for the equally bold structure of evergreen cottage favourite box (*Buxus sempervirens*) and statuesque *Cynara cardunculus* to show just how dramatic and exciting a garden can be when plantings from two different styles of garden collide.

summer if there is no rain for several weeks. I also mulch with recycled green waste or well-rotted farmyard manure annually to reduce the need for watering and to condition the soil."

Another rule was that the plants must be able to grow well without staking, so that they are easy to manage. Many plants, such as *Achillea filipendulina* 'Gold Plate', nepeta, and *Persicaria microcephala* 'Red Dragon', are cut back in spring to prevent them from becoming leggy and to eliminate the need for support.

And the final rule was that the plants should have interesting foliage where possible. This would extend the season of interest and create a multitude of contrasts and textures. A combination of *Nandina domestica* and *Alstroemeria* Indian Summer is an example of her use of vibrant flower and foliage effect.

Jenny also knew that the garden had to stand up to close scrutiny in winter because most of it can be viewed from the house. Therefore foliage from evergreens would have to play a big part in keeping the winter scenery looking good from inside.

In this part of the UK, the winters tend to be mild and largely frost-free, so the hoar frosts that would show off the skeletons in a new perennial planting in winter are sadly lacking. Instead Jenny relies more on evergreens to keep the garden looking appealing in winter.

A succession of *Stipa gigantea* plantings and box balls provided the initial backbone for the garden, with groupings of perennials in fives and sevens knitting together around them over time. And the low habit of *Phlomis russeliana*, another effective evergreen, makes it ideal for smothering weeds.

Grasses planted throughout the garden have proved invaluable for providing a continuous backdrop, keeping the garden looking full and interesting through winter. In summer *Calamagrostis ×acutiflora* 'Karl Foerster' is a top pick for drought-tolerance, not receiving any water at all, while *Miscanthus sinensis* 'Ferner Osten' provides movement to the back of the border when its tall flower stalks sway in the summer wind.

The borders are on show from all angles, and although they are mostly viewed through bifold doors that run the length of the house, being able to sit in the garden was another must. So Jenny uses the trick of placing a seating area where you can be enveloped by the plants, as does Piet Oudolf in the perennial meadow at Scampston Walled Garden. "I wanted to create a feel of sanctuary and of the plants enveloping you," Jenny said.

Having extreme conditions and starting with challenging soil in the garden at Churt Lea Cottage makes it important to create plant communities, targeting plants that naturally occur in similar places in the wild. Jenny realized that plants that thrive in a Mediterranean climate, such as alstroemerias, phlomis, anthemis, and *Salvia nemorosa* 'Caradonna' were a good fit with the light, free-draining soil and sunny site.

To identify and fill gaps in the garden, Jenny is a big advocate of taking pictures at different times of year, and she uses bulbs to plug obvious gaps that she identifies, with alliums and species tulips being her preferred choices to fit in with the style of the garden. These are also perennial, making a more permanent feature in the garden than the more ephemeral hybrid tulips.

Robust and upright flowering *Salvia nemorosa* 'Caradonna' provides the perfect partner for the airy and loose, golden flowers of self-seeding California poppies, providing an eye-catching contrast of colour and shape.

Jenny plants catmint around perennial tulips because the timing of the catmint bursting into life coincides with when the tulip finishes flowering and needs something to cover its dying foliage.

Not all plant selections have struck gold here, however. 'Goldsturm' rudbeckia simply couldn't cope with the dry summers and broke the watering rule that Jenny had set, but she just saw this as an opportunity to try something else:

*There are so many plants that I can't even contemplate growing in this soil, but I do like to experiment. I like to try and push the boundaries of what can be grown. You sometimes have to be ruthless. It seems a very British thing to try and eek out the existence of a plant. Sometimes you just have to replace struggling plants with something new.*

And that's the essence of the modern cottage garden.

# In Small Spaces

Don't be daunted by majestic swathes of new perennial plantings or sprawling cottage garden borders: you can recreate their magic in a smaller space—in a new modern cottage garden. If you have seen either of the component styles at a flower show or in a large private garden open to the public, pick out a combination or a trio of plants that look good together and they will probably end up having even more impact at home.

The traditional English cottage garden style has an air of untidiness about it, a natural inclination to allow plants to scramble, spread, and seed around to create a fulsome garden. The new perennial style, although aiming to look as if plants have naturalized, is in truth a little more ordered, with blocks of planting knitted together.

In small spaces it makes sense to rein in how free-flowing the garden can look. Otherwise the most vigorous plants can take up too high a proportion of the space and leave the garden lacking in diversity.

Nothing is more obvious than when a garden depends too much on one or two plants, especially in a small space. It's a bit like a club where the same two people do all the organizing, leaving no room for new and exciting ideas. If when you walk out into a small garden your eyes are instantly drawn to one plant because it is spreading through and over others, then the chances are that the whole is worth less than the sum of its parts and this will not result in an exciting garden in a small space. In small spaces,

Variegated ivies and *Erigeron karvinskianus* will gently cascade over border edges and can be easily controlled in small spaces, with grasses planted among them to add height to the display.

a plant that self-seeds freely, such as *Erigeron karvinskianus*, may seem like a novelty at first but if allowed to run free uncontrollably, it can soon hog too much of the stage.

To avoid the same plants taking over around the boundaries of the garden, plant climbers two by two, so that they can cover a wall or trellis together. We are unlikely to plant up a whole flowerbed or border with the same plant, yet we think nothing of clothing a large wall with just one climbing plant. Our expectations of the boundaries in the garden should be as high as of the planting at ground level where space is at a premium.

Also don't be afraid to plant tall, flamboyant grasses such as *Calama-grostis ×acutiflora* 'Karl Foerster' around the base of climbers to help them blend into the borders and create intriguing colour combinations. For an autumn light show, try planting climbers with colourful autumn leaves such as *Parthenocissus quinquefolia* (Virginia creeper) behind the ageing foliage of grasses.

If there are plants in the garden that self-seed, assess how many you can keep at the seedling stage in spring and then be ruthless. In a limited space, not every plant that pops up can stay. Allowing every seedling that germinates in a border to stay and then having too much of one plant is a bit like allowing a child to do your food shopping for you and then wondering why they've come back with a basket full of candy and not much else. You can have too much of a good thing no matter what the merits of a plant may be.

Another consideration when space is limited is that you don't have to allow plants to grow to their maximum height and spread. If you have your heart set on a particular shrub or rose, then it can always be controlled by pruning. With perennials it is not so easy because the

Be selective when deciding how many self-seeded plants to keep in the garden or the space can be swamped by one plant. Here a concentrated patch of pot marigolds has been controlled so that there is room for purple salvias and pink *Lychnis coronaria* to grow alongside them in harmony.

Small spring-flowering plants such as saxifrages or aubrietas are useful for fitting into small gaps to provide extra flowers and some old-fashioned charm to evergreen perennials such as *Euphorbia amygdaloides* 'Purpurea' and evergreen grasses.

plants grow from scratch each year rather than increasing in size incrementally year by year, although regular division can reduce the spread of the plant.

Adding seasonal plants into tiny gaps is another easy way to get the most from limited space. There are lots of small, spring-flowering perennials such as saxifrages and aubrietas that can add a pretty, old-fashioned flourish in tiny gaps. They are especially useful among established evergreens that can be lonely in spring while many plants are still dormant or yet to burst into leaf or flower.

## PLANT COMBINATIONS FOR DRAMA IN SMALL SPACES

We live in a world where the mantra "more for less" surrounds many of us post financial crashes. Although this may be regrettable in some areas of society, we would do well to consider this approach in the garden when space is severely limited. Look around the garden at the established plants that take up the most space and ask yourself if there is room for two different plants where you currently have just one.

Finding opportunities to grow a wider range of plants can be the start of trying out the modern cottage garden style. A traditional herbaceous border plant grown in isolation can be transformed by planting a contrasting new perennial next to it and vice versa. Established clumps of herbaceous perennials can be lifted and divided in early spring or autumn to reduce the plants' spread and allow for a new plant next to it or even in the middle of the clump.

Planting around the edge of other plants is a good way to incorporate spring bulbs into a planting scheme. Try pairing them with perennials that have attractive foliage in spring, such as *Pulmonaria* 'Trevi Fountain' or *Brunnera macrophylla* 'Jack Frost', to create a layered display.

Adding height to the garden around the margins of lower-growing plants is also an easy way to make a big impact with two plants where before there was only space for one. The hollyhock, one of the most gorgeous of all the classic cottage garden plants, grows superbly in soil that drains well, tolerating drought exceptionally. Plants that produce flowers neatly on slim stems will add lots of impact in a tight space, and there may be none neater than this cottage garden classic. Also try planting some around the edges of dome-shaped perennials such as *Euphorbia characias* or any of the hardy perennial sedums for a mix of old and new at different heights. Also plant them with tall grasses for an ethereal blend of traditional flowers and contemporary texture.

Another plant with slender flower stems that is useful for squeezing into a mixed planting when space is tight is the rather underused *Sisyrinchium striatum*. Where I grew up, it had the rather unflattering common name of pigroot, which sounded more like an animal feed or

**Above:** Heucheras are a cottage garden favourite and take up little room in a border but create a big impact when in flower, especially when grown against solid backdrops such as the fulsome strands of evergreen grass *Stipa tenuissima*.

**Below:** *Brunnera macrophylla* 'Jack Frost' is a beautiful short groundcover plant for edging a border with its silvery patterned leaves, and a bold, warm-coloured grass such as *Imperata cylindrica* 'Rubra' will help the foliage stand out all summer long. In a small space, pittosporums such as *P. tenuifolium* 'Variegatum' make gorgeous background shrubs that can be pruned during the growing season to keep them in their allotted space.

a foul-smelling weed than a pretty perennial (but that's common plant names for you). Its spires of dainty flowers, cream with a buttery yellow centre, are a real summer treat and reach a similar height to wispy strands of *Stipa tenuissima* and many achilleas. Sisyrinchiums can freely self seed, but it's just a case of being selective, taking out the ones you don't want and transplanting the ones you do to an advantageous position in spring. It is a splendid foil for short wispy grasses in a small space, and because of its fairly short, unobtrusive leaves it can be planted among grasses so that the two can appear as if they were one plant.

**Above:** Plants with neat, slim, flowering stems such as catmint (*Nepeta*) are the perfect subjects for growing among other plants where their flowers can weave in to create contrasts in colour and texture in a small space.

**Above right:** The upright habit of euphorbias makes them useful plants to squeeze into gaps in borders. With their long season of interest they can star in spring, teaming up with the cheerful spring flowers of saxifrages, as well as with the upright bright pink flowers of bergenias such as 'Bressingham Ruby'.

**Right:** The dark and moody leaves and flowers of hardy *Geranium phaeum* var. *phaeum* 'Samobor' in the middle of this planting are softened by *Stipa tenuissima* to create a full and intricately textured pocket of garden in a small space in full sun or semi-shade in well-drained soil. The geranium spreads to just 45cm (1ft 6in) wide and the stipa to just 50cm (1ft 8in).

The spires of creamy yellow flowers of *Sisyrinchium striatum* pop up among wispy strands of grasses such as *Imperata cylindrica* 'Rubra' or *Carex buchananii*, and they also provide a fresh foil for more intense summer flowers such as achilleas and salvias which show their best flower colour in full sun, in soil that drains very well.

# More plant combinations for small spaces

It's not easy teaming plants together when space is tight, especially if each individual plant is to be shown off at its best. But it can be done effectively with some careful plant selection. Here are some plant duos that won't demand too much space, while looking effective together.

Catmint, with its loose growing habit, is perfectly suited to nestling among grasses in a border to make good use of the space. It is also a natural to have around silver-leaved plants such as this artemisia (bottom right) to create a cool colour combination in summer in a warm, dry spot.

With their branching flower stems, eryngiums contrast well with perennials that bear slender flowers on upright stems. There always seems to be room in the garden for *Salvia nemorosa* 'Caradonna' which will squeeze into a gap by an eryngium and enjoy growing in the free-draining soil and full sun that both need in order to thrive.

The starry clusters of *Sedum* 'Matrona' colour the border edges boldly in autumn and provide architectural interest earlier in the year with their blood-red stems and glaucous blue-green leaves. Partner them with giant *Allium cristophii* flowers, which will add intricate patterning in a small space, flowering in May and showing sculptural interest until winter. Grow both in a sunny spot in well-drained soil.

For daisy-like flowers all summer long, *Anthemis tinctoria* 'Wargave Variety' is a compact and tidy plant that grows to just 90cm (3ft) tall in the border, making the perfect platform in a small space for a short perennial with sprawling flower stems such as *Sanguisorba officinalis*. Grow both in a sunny spot in well-drained soil.

Keep deadheading *Dahlia merckii* and it will flower all summer in full sun and until the first hard frost arrives at the end of the growing season. Its tiny, purple-pink flowers are daintier and more refined than many of the brasher *Dahlia* varieties and its spindly flower stems—around 1.2m (4ft) tall—stand out well against a solid backdrop of intense colour provided by magenta-flowered *Salvia nemorosa* 'Schwellenburg'.

Japanese anemones are rapidly spreading perennials but valuable for their late flowers that show throughout autumn, flowering well in semi-shade. *Anemone ×hybrida* 'Elegans' reaches 1.2m (4ft) tall, and although it will spread quickly, it is a fine plant for blending with grasses because its flower stems are held well above their leaves, allowing them to mix with the nodding flowers of stipas, such as *Stipa gigantea* 'Gold Fontaene', and molinias. All grow well in moist, well-drained soil.

*Echinacea purpurea* and *Sporobolus heterolepis* will look good in the garden from summer until winter when the shades of orange and brown on the seedheads of the echinacea are lightened by the fine and feathery straw-coloured silhouettes of the sporobolus flowers. Grow them in a sunny, well-drained spot in the garden.

You could be forgiven for thinking that a large border is needed for a combination such as this one growing in the garden at Dove Cottage Nursery in Halifax, UK, but it will add big impact in a tight spot of well-drained soil in full sun. *Echinacea purpurea* 'Pink Glow' sends up sturdy flower stems with flat, almost horizontal flowers that provide the perfect contrast with the tall, wiry *Veronicastrum virginicum* 'Erica' which although grand and statuesque at 1.2m (4ft) tall will only spread to around 60cm (2ft).

Grasses with arching flower stems and foliage are especially good for adding another dimension to an area of planting, seen here growing at Dove Cottage Nursery, creating a shimmering smokescreen among bolder flowers such as those of *Persicaria* species. Varieties of *Molinia caerulea* subsp. *arundinacea* such as 'Black Arrows' are especially useful in a small space because they form a narrow, neat mound of foliage with the dark brown flowers appearing as if from nowhere in summer and providing structure through winter.

# RECONSIDER THE LAWN

The lawn is a mainstay of many traditional gardens, and also features in some notable examples of the new perennial garden, namely the Millennium borders planted by Piet Oudolf at the Royal Horticultural Society Garden, Wisley, in the UK.

So the modern cottage garden can work both with and without a lawn. For some gardeners, the idea of not having an area of grass in the garden is out of the question, perhaps because it keeps a partner occupied and out of the way while there is some real gardening to be done! Or maybe it is the therapeutic process of creating straight lines with a lawnmower.

Of course lawns bring a lot to a garden, not least a soft carpet to sit and walk on and an expanse of green all the year. Often we forget that lawn grasses are evergreen plants and the healthiest-looking subjects in the whole garden in winter and that they can look better in winter and spring that at any other time.

But do you truly need a lawn in your garden? Regularly mowing a lawn can become a chore and also a problem if the garden has to be left for any length of time because once it gets away from you it can be hard work to get it back. Who wants to get back from a holiday to tackle hours of mowing and raking up grass clippings? In small spaces a lawn is a luxury: having a monoculture in a small garden comes at the expense of the diversity that can be enjoyed through mixing together different textures and colours of planting.

If the lawn doesn't serve a practical purpose in the garden, such as a soccer pitch for the kids or a well-used soft landing for some sunbathing, then consider reducing it to a network of grass paths to demarcate planting areas.

A sinuous, windy path does a grand job of showing off plants that naturally cascade over the edges to add a natural flow and to make the garden look bigger, especially if you place a sundial, statue, or tree at the end of it. Try edging a path with lime-green cascading grass *Hakonechloa macra* 'Aureola' or fresh, pale green and white *Molinia caerulea* subsp. *caerulea* 'Variegata'. You will be surprisingly grateful for the greenery

Think about how much a lawn adds to the look of the garden and then decide if it is worth the constant maintenance from spring to autumn.

a lawn path provides in a temperate winter when it makes a sharp contrast with the monochrome colouring of old perennial plants.

Soil conditions can also help you make the decision of whether to have a lawn. If your soil is heavy, then grass paths that are well used will quickly become compacted, leaving you with a hard, bare area in summer and a wet, boggy area in winter. A gravel path in its place will look good all year round and will greatly improve drainage too.

# Ways to make garden spaces seem bigger

If a keen gardener was granted one gardening wish, would it be more time or more space? I'm sure many of us would opt for the latter, so here are some handy ideas for making the space that you have in the garden seem bigger than it actually is and making the maximum use of it.

**Add seating at every opportunity.** Squeeze as many seating areas (this one can be found at Dove Cottage Nursery in Halifax, UK) into your garden as possible and you will have more parts of the garden that get viewed at close quarters. By sitting around different parts of the garden you will also get up close and personal with far more of it and end up with a more intimate knowledge of even tiny parts of the garden. When you begin to notice the abundance of life in the tiniest of spaces, the whole garden will seem like a much bigger place.

**Make paths sinuous.** Whether you edge a path with a beautiful dome of fully double roses or an arching fountain of plumage from a prairie grass, the effect will be most dramatic if the paths wind around the edges of the plants. And just like driving along windy roads tends to make journeys longer and more interesting than driving on straight ones, so the same can be said for a border path that bends and conceals what is around the corner.

**Hide the end of the garden.** Use a hedge, wall, trellis, or an area of tall plants to hide the boundaries of the garden. Even if the garden doesn't extend much further behind these barriers, they will add a layer of intrigue—what lies beyond?— and will separate the garden into rooms, each with its own atmosphere.

**Lead the eye to the horizon.** Make your borders tail off to a narrow point. This is a simple trick if you want borders with a straight rather than a curvy edge and works best if you've got borders that face each other. Place a gap in a hedge or a pergola at the point where the two ends meet.

### Group containers together to make false borders.

If the garden has a lot of hard surfaces, try grouping together your containers along the edges to make an extra bonus border. You can have great fun with this as you mix and match different pots to create new planting combinations. And if some don't work, just keep swapping the pots around until you settle on something that you like. The beauty of this is that plants with completely opposite growing needs, such as poor-soil-thriving lavender, can be positioned alongside moisture-loving plants such as astrantia and astilbe. In my garden this allows for drought-loving euphorbias, which grow well in thin soil, to grow alongside roses, which prefer heavier, bulkier soils. I also pair hebes, which grow well in light soil and full sun, with roses and grasses such as *Carex oshimensis* 'Eversheen', which prefers a soil that is always moist.

### Go vertical.

What place do hanging baskets have in the modern cottage garden? A basket of loud-coloured annuals may seem light years away from the style, but with a bit of imagination and some perennial planting, they can blend in with the borders nearby. Similarly, hanging a mirror in the garden is a cunning way to have multiples of the same plant without growing it in more than one place. Install a mirror and you can have a magnificent flowerbed or container display that seems to be at both ends of the garden. Mirrors work really well if you have a wall facing a flowerbed or a packed area of containers. Fix it to a wall or solid structure and you'll be able to see the garden from a whole new perspective. Soften the edges of the mirror by growing plants around it for a further layer of intrigue to the garden. Avoid positioning a mirror along flight-paths used by garden birds.

# In Containers

Being restricted to container growing is often seen as a negative thing, with anybody that declares that they only have space to grow plants in pots subjected to words of sympathy and sadness, as if they had just announced that they do not have a roof over their heads. Yet growing plants in containers is a tremendous opportunity to grow plants together to create a definite garden style. When you mix together a range of carefully selected plants, differences in leaf textures and colours can be exaggerated and shown in a way that may not be possible in a crowded garden border.

To make the most of small spaces on a patio or in a yard where container growing is the only option, growing multiple plants in the same pot is the best way to make the space look like a viable garden with a style of its own, rather than just being a collection of random specimens in containers. Squeezing an extra plant into a container can also be a good way to make the modern cottage style work. A pot of new perennial plants can be given an extra flourish by the inclusion of an old-fashioned container staple. Try edging a pot of prairie perennials with a well-behaved trailing plant such as a calibrachoa to bridge the two styles.

**Above left:** Mixing plants together in containers allows for all manner of new perennial and cottage garden favourites to be grown together to make exciting and stylish displays. In my own garden it allows me to add extra layers of detail into a small area to make the most of the space.

**Far left:** Planting a container with plants in flower is a good way of being sure that you are happy with the combination and takes away the uncertainty of how the display will look.

**Left:** Simply adding a drought-tolerant calibrachoa to the edge of a pot of perennials makes the planting work harder in the garden and adds extra summer-long colour in a tight space.

# CONTAINER-PLANTING BASICS

Yes, of course plants in pots tend to be higher maintenance than plants growing in the ground but having to be in a daily routine of checking containers opens up our eyes to notice the intricacies of how plants change on a daily basis. It increases our awareness of the changing seasons and helps us notice the idiosyncrasies of individual plants that we can easily miss if the plant is simply planted and forgotten in a border. If you truly want to get to know a plant, grow it in a pot.

Plants in containers can also be forgiving at times if daily attention isn't possible. They won't demand daily watering unless a summer is exceptionally hot and dry, so long as they are grown in the right compost and the plants are watered in the cool of the evening or early morning. Wandering out into the garden at the end of a warm summer's day to water plants growing in pots is one of the joys of gardening.

Most plants in containers will grow well in a mixture of equal parts multipurpose compost and soil-based compost mixed together. Avoid just planting in multipurpose compost alone: it contains only a few weeks' supply of nutrients for the plants, shrinks over time, and can be very poor at holding onto water.

Plants that thrive on lighter soils will benefit from the addition of horticultural grit to the mix. Plants that prefer acidic soil can be grown in soil-based, lime-free, John Innes compost mixed with equal parts ericaceous compost. (John Innes refers to a set of basic formulas for making compost, not to a brand.)

Plants that thrive in heavy clay or boggy soil need something heavy that will hold onto moisture well so are best planted with soil-based compost only, which will retain moisture incredibly well. Just remember that it will make the container heavy, so it is best to place the pot where you want it to stay before planting it up.

If you are unsure of the way that plants will blend in a container, choose plants in flower that are looking their best rather than plants that are small and establishing and won't look good or mature until the following year. Place them in a trolley at the plant centre and mix and match them until you hit upon a combination that you like.

Before you buy, though, make sure that the plants have similar soil requirements and that the pot you choose can accommodate the plants without the rootballs having to be squashed (it's not just humans who can feel claustrophobic). If you are struggling to decide which size pot to choose for a mixed display, always err on the side of a pot that is too big, because you can never have too much space in a mixed container.

Plant the container in the evening, water it very well, and keep it in shade for the first couple of days if you are planting up plants in flower in summer or early autumn. This allows the plants to settle before they are exposed to warm conditions.

Follow these principles, and the plants will be off to a good start.

A mix of equal parts multipurpose compost and soil-based compost will provide weight and nutrients to your container.

## MAKING A MODERN COTTAGE GARDEN WITH CONTAINERS

Growing plants in containers also allows for the garden to be portable. If you are one of those people who like to move the furniture in your living room on a regular basis, then you are probably wise to this trick of swapping the positions of the pots in your yard. Moving containers around through the year to create different colour combinations is great fun and opens up the mind to figuring out a display in the garden that excites you.

A concrete yard or patio can become a container border, where a selection of mixed pots is arranged to create what appears to be an herbaceous border. If you have some old favourites such as roses growing alone in pots and grasses in pots, then you can instantly get a flavour of what the modern cottage garden can bring to your outdoor space.

Arrange plants in pots to make a container border that will bring definition to a concrete yard or patio.

**Overleaf:** Grouping together plants in containers helps soften path edges and allows for mini-borders to be made on hard surfaces, as seen in the garden at 39 Foster Road, Cambridgeshire, UK.

And the beauty of this way of growing is that plants can be paired together that wouldn't necessarily grow in the same patch of soil. Yet grow them in two separate containers, each with different composts and drainage, and you can truly cheat nature. So clay-hungry roses can grow in containers of heavy, soil-based compost, while lovers of free drainage such as echinaceas and lavender can be grown in a mix of multipurpose and soil-based composts mixed with horticultural grit. But they can sit beside each other, and if the containers are artfully arranged, the plants will look like they are all growing in the same place.

However, to see the potential of the modern cottage garden in containers, plant different kinds of plants in the same vessel to get a greater depth of colour and more diversity in growth habits and leaf detail. A collection of containers like these placed together looks more like a border than if you group together lots of plants planted singly in pots.

To create a border-style display with containers, adding plants that gently tumble over the edge of the pots is a must. These could be classic annual trailing plants such as calibrachoa and trailing pelargoniums, or something subtler such as a grass that gracefully arches over the rim of the pot. Try a variegated carex such as Everest or even a broad-leaved wood rush (*Luzula sylvatica*) for something not as understated.

Containers can also be cunningly placed around the edge of beds and borders in the garden to soften the transition between the different elements or to create a plant combination that wouldn't be possible in the same patch of soil in the ground. Pots can also mask empty areas in winter if they contain evergreens or other plants with effective winter structure.

**Above:** Place containers against border and path edges to soften the transitions. Pots with evergreen perennials, grasses, and shrubs will keep the garden looking full even in winter. The whole of my garden is visible from indoors which makes year-round appeal desirable because there is no hiding place for any part of the garden— it is on show all year.

**Above:** Siting containers around the edge of a raised bed softens the edge and blends with the adjacent planting.

**Left:** Mix and match your pots along the edge of a building or pathway to create a moveable backyard border that can be augmented with new displays each season to ensure there is always colour and interest.

## MAKE A MODERN HANGING BASKET

An essential element of a traditional English garden, hanging baskets make for the perfect welcome by a front door or porch in summer; in a small garden they can also draw the eye upward and maximize available space.

Unfortunately hanging basket planting is often limited to a narrow range of tender plants that flower from summer to the frosts and although these plants are useful, there are so many more opportunities available when it comes to what to plant in them.

There are many exciting combinations for hanging baskets that venture beyond the usual suspects of petunias, fuchsias, and busy lizzies or impatiens. As well as providing an opportunity to mix perennials with more familiar annual bedding plants, baskets are also the ideal home for

**From left:**

Plant hanging baskets with plants that can tolerate drought and they no longer have to be a high-maintenance garden feature.

Potentillas are a popular cottage garden perennial for full sun, and they are perfectly at home with an echeveria, a sempervivum, and a delosperma in a drought-tolerant hanging basket.

A year-round hanging basket containing a drought-tolerant mix of catmint, sedums, rosemary, and ivy draws the eye upward and adds a cozy touch to my small back garden. It needs little watering and no feeding; the only routine maintenance is deadheading and trimming of any stems that have trailed further than you want them to.

growing drought-tolerant plants, making a low-maintenance feature out of something that is notoriously high-maintenance.

Try centrepiece plants that could also feature in the border such as catmint (*Nepeta*) or *Carex oshimensis* 'Evergold' and the display will be linked to the rest of the garden. Old cottage garden staples rosemary and lavender can also make good centrepieces and their tolerance of drought is useful during hot summers when watering containers can seem like a full-time job.

Don't worry about some plants getting too big when you grow small perennials or shrubs in baskets. Any shrubs can be pruned to keep them compact and perennials removed and divided after the first year if they start to take up too much room.

# My Modern Cottage Container Garden

## Hull, UK

Welcome to my tiny garden in Hull, UK.

When we first viewed it, I told my wife that we could not possibly live here because the garden was too small (at 8.5m × 2.7m or 28ft × 9ft), but with our options dwindling and our need of a permanent place to stay after moving north from London, we duly arrived. Winter was biting, the temperature was well below freezing, and a week after we moved in, the garden was filled up with empty removal boxes and covered in snow.

However, once spring warmly and suddenly arrived in early April, I began to realize that although gardening in small spaces can be frustrating, it also has many advantages. This ended up being the perfect place to create a modern cottage garden.

Even in the garden's first year, tall perennials in pots such as *Echinacea purpurea* 'Magnus' add height and interest to an entrance.

The garden when I arrived was just the bare bones with very little soil to plant in. It was a blank canvas, but this opens up a world of opportunities. To reach the soil in the far corner of the garden, I removed the stones and concrete base from the raised beds, then topped up the soil level before planting in spring.

In this view also taken just fifteen months after being planted up from scratch, the whole space is starting to show off the strength of the modern cottage garden in summer: a vibrant mix of exciting evergreen plants in pots; a tapestry of perennials and shrubs with colourful and patterned leaves; a mix of colourful early summer flowers mingling with slender grasses; and the promise of a lot more colour and structure to come in the rest of summer and beyond.

**Left:** Towards the end of the first summer, there is good structure from erysimums, *Stipa tenuissima*, and evergreen shrubs and grasses, while rudbeckias and roses provide the bulk of the colour and trailing ivies help to give the garden an informal feel. Orange-flowered pot marigolds (*Calendula officinalis*) sown direct in the soil in spring prove invaluable gap fillers for the bed at the end of the garden.

**Below:** By the start of the second summer, plantings in the raised beds and containers soften the hard edges of the garden, and tinted woodstain provides an extra flourish of colour. Here in early summer there are lots of strong colours to enjoy, with richer reds and yellows to follow later in the season. There is a solid structure of evergreen planting knitting everything together, to ensure that the garden looks fresh and full, whatever the time of year.

Roses that produce several flushes of flowers such as pink Boscobel and coppery orange 'Lady of Shalott' are invaluable in a small space and are the perfect subjects for planting in front of an old brick wall to effortlessly create that feeling of old-fashioned charm in the garden.

I have talked about nostalgia influencing many plant choices in the garden, and so it was for me. My first job out of college was working for a rose grower, and ever since then I have had a soft spot for these plants. So roses were must-have plants for the garden. Fortunately many recently introduced roses are a great improvement on the roses that gardeners remember from their childhood or their grandparents' garden. Warm coppery orange 'Lady of Shalott' and warm pink Boscobel roses flower continuously from early summer to the end of autumn and barely shed a leaf over winter in my garden, let alone develop any disease on the leaves. They also have exceptional scent. There has truly never been a better time to grow roses in the garden.

My plan once the roses were planted was to weave other plants among them to cover their "bare legs" and to mingle among their stems—something that is particularly important when the roses are in their first year and their stems are not as sturdy as they will be in future seasons. Integral in this were variegated ivies, calibrachoas, and evergreen grasses *Stipa tenuissima* and *Carex oshimensis* Everest.

The whole of the garden can be viewed from both the kitchen and the dining room of the house so I soon also realized that the garden needed a good evergreen backbone to provide form, texture, and colour through the year. Evergreen grasses were a must, both in the ground and in containers, and euphorbias became invaluable for providing height to containers and bringing a diverse mix of colour and texture to the garden all through the year.

**Clockwise from top left:**

Evergreen grass such as *Carex oshimensis* Everest have been essential for providing form and structure to soften the edges of the garden. They also make fine companions for cottage garden plants such as roses and erysimums. Just remember to split them up in spring because they multiply quickly.

Every tiny bit of space counts in my garden, and having colourful plants such as this lime-green–leaved 'Sweet Tart' heuchera to brighten up the smallest of gaps under other plants (here, a 'Princess Anne' rose) helps get maximum impact from the space available.

Plants with eye-catching foliage can create a beautifully textured understory beneath taller plants and a feeling of fullness and diversity in a small garden. Areas beneath large roses tend to be shady, which is perfect for spotty leaved *Pulmonaria* 'Trevi Fountain', silver-leaved *Brunnera macrophylla* 'Jack Frost', and variegated ivy. Golden carex lifts the scene with some bolder colour, and lavender and fuchsias provide more colour in a container where the shade is not so heavy.

Once the roses and the evergreens were in place—most of the garden's largest plants—it was then time to fill in the gaps with smaller plants to tie everything together. Covering bare spaces in the first year of a garden is always a challenge. You need bridging plants that provide colour and structure while you wait for other plants to get established that will eventually form the garden's backbone.

In the first year when there was no additional room for growing direct in the soil, empty areas around entrances were crying out for containers to enliven the space. Climbers are the obvious choice around a doorway, but while I was waiting for them to grow tall enough to fill in their space, I tried some containers of tall perennials for big impact. *Echinacea purpurea* 'Magnus' helped to cheer up the area around the garden's back door. It grows to at least a meter tall and with the added elevation of the container, it provided height.

Another invaluable bridging plant was that cottage garden classic pot marigold (*Calendula officinalis*). It is a tremendously fast-growing annual that I sowed direct into the soil in spring. It flowered non-stop from around the end of June until the first frosts, and in true cottage garden style, it scrambles through a border. The variety I grew reached around 1.2m (4ft) tall and proved incredibly useful for providing bright colour and bushiness to the garden in the first year while other perennials were trying to get established.

As well as endeavouring to overcome a lack of space and an initial feeling of bareness in year one, I also faced another potential problem: shade. The garden sits in the shade of some mature trees from the cemetery over the back wall, and the house and the garden walls cast some parts of the garden in shade for most of the day all year round. Rather than just focus on woodland plants often recommended for shade, I thought it would be worthwhile to push the boundaries and see what else would grow well in heavy shade.

Although a lot of plants prefer sun, you can still grow them in shade. There is a false impression that plants will drop down dead if they are not grown where it states on the label. But although they might not produce as many flowers, they are less affected by hot spells and need less watering. Shrub rose Lady Emma

**Below left:** Areas of heavy shade don't have to be a problem. This is the shadiest part of the garden, receiving little sun at all, but it is also the lushest part, with clematis, ivy, hollyhocks, euphorbias, and orange *Erysimum* 'Apricot Twist' looking fresh all through summer in both hot and cool spells.

**Below:** A mix of orange pot marigold 'Princess Orange Black', Halo Mix hollyhock, 'Magnus' echinacea, and Lady Emma Hamilton roses growing well in almost full shade in my garden.

*Erysimum* 'Bowles's Mauve' is a cottage garden favourite and with its long flowering season and evergreen leaves, it has become a reliable, long-blooming stalwart in the garden. It blends beautifully with old-fashioned clematis and with the variegated grass *Phalaris arundinacea* var. *picta* 'Feesey'.

Hamilton grew well in deep shade and still had two flushes of orange-to-red flowers, and heleniums and echinacea coped admirably in a spot receiving a maximum of around two hours sun a day in high summer.

The majority of the garden is concrete yard so growing plants in containers and grouping them together to mimic an area of planted garden became an essential trick. This enclosed the garden and softened the edges (which are brick on all sides).

Planting lots of mixed containers with more than one plant also helped the garden look consistent on all sides. Plants at the back and right-hand side of the garden are growing in the ground while the left-hand side is all container plants. Leaving gaps between the containers and planting them with single plants would have made the garden lop-sided with an obvious difference between the borders at the back and on the right and the yard area on the left. Instead I opted for the three sides to all tie in together to make a stronger whole.

The use of coloured woodstain for the garden furniture and raised beds was a finishing touch to give the garden some year-round colour that complements the flowering plants in summer and autumn. Using one colour all over also helps to keep the garden unified and draws the eye to see the garden as a whole, rather than as a fragmented space. I paint the furniture and raised beds a different colour each year, though, so that pictures of the garden in different years can be easily compared and also to keep the garden looking fresh and distinctive. It is easy for a small garden to seem too familiar because of lack of space.

The woodstained furniture and raised beds are also something of a more modern feature to contrast with the rustic brick wall, another way of incorporating the old with the new to emphasize the forming of a new style.

# FEATURE CONTAINERS

If space on the patio is limited, or you need the space for entertaining or children's games (a book on soccer-friendly plants is perhaps a good idea for the future) then the sparing use of some feature containers can still bring modern cottage garden style to your yard. This is an opportunity to group together some of the hardest-working, longest-flowering plants that blend together well to create a mini-garden in a pot. Think of it as an at-a-glance summing up of the style.

A healthy rose that will produce four or even five flushes of flowers throughout the season is a good starting point. A variety such as 'Maid Marion' is a good candidate. It has tasteful mid-pink flowers with one of the sharpest scents you can get from a rose. It will hold onto its leaves all the way through the autumn and into winter, only dropping its leaves when temperatures consistently fall below freezing. Then it will be business as usual in spring. Other good rose candidates for containers include tall and very bushy English rose Vanessa Bell, with scented, lemon yellow flowers. It is one of the healthiest roses you can grow and is surprisingly tolerant of dry conditions.

Rudbeckias make good neighbours for roses in containers because they both like a soil that stays moist at all times through the summer. 'Goldsturm' is a classic rudbeckia and rightly so because it is a neat grower (always an advantage when growing more than one plant in a pot) and its flowers are long-lasting and weather-proof, looking good until the end of fall, with the added bonus of providing some structure which can look pretty if caught by hoar frost.

A plant to provide colour at the edge of the pot makes a nice finishing touch and adds an informal flourish to the pot, which echoes the laid-back nature of the modern cottage garden, calibrachoas will start flowering in summer and keep going until temperatures fall below 10°C (50°F), while *Erigeron karvinskianus* is hardy and will highlight the edges of the pot with neat daisy flowers all through summer. Gaps at the edges can be filled in winter with ivies (which are at their best in pots because they won't run rampant and colonize a large area so easily).

Having at least one grass in a feature pot will greatly enhance the season of interest, as well as adding height, movement, and fullness to the finish. If space is tight, try one with wispy leaves such as *Carex comans* bronze-leaved, which can weave itself between other large plants without getting squashed.

Euphorbias are also invaluable in feature pots because of their ability to look outstanding, whatever month of the year is showing up on the calendar. *Euphorbia amygdaloides* 'Purpurea' is among the most generous. In spring its bronze-purple leaves add rich, almost autumn-like colour to the scene before unleashing bright lime-green bracts to contrast with louder flowers and emerging leaf shoots. Then in winter it is the perfect partner to fill out the gaps between grasses.

# How to plant a colourful spring container step-by-step

Mixed containers can transform a patio area. Think of them as permanent fixtures—just as permanent in the garden as trees or shrubs—so it is worth taking time to plant them up. Getting the compost, planting levels, and planting partners right will pay off in the long run and give pleasure for years to come.

1. Choose plants with a mixture of heights to add depth and structure to your container display. This will make it like a mini-border or garden in a pot and will allow you to show off the best features of each plant well.

2. For containers with plants that require well-drained soil (such as this collection of euphorbias, saxifrages, and erysimums) add three trowels full of grit to a large container and mix it into the compost thoroughly.

5. Tease apart congested roots at the base of the rootball of your plants. You can be surprisingly heavy-handed with fibrous-rooted plants such as this *Euphorbia amygdaloides* 'Purpurea'. Rip the roots and spread them out. If you have to, you can also gently squash plant rootballs of well-rooted plants to help the plants fit in the container. Gently, mind!

6. Once you have your layout, sprinkle compost into the gaps until the roots are all covered. Firm the compost with your hands as you go to eliminate air pockets and help anchor the plants.

7. Move the pot to its final position, then water the whole of the compost surface gently to avoid splashing the leaves. Stop watering when puddles start to form on the compost surface.

8. Once the water has drained from the compost surface, sprinkle a layer of decorative mulch over all the bare compost to smarten the container and help keep the plant's roots cool in summer.

9. The finished container (see next page) promises the bright, fresh colours of spring but will go on to provide colour and structure to the patio right through the year, with the erysimum flowering all summer until first frosts, the carex providing year-round architecture, and the euphorbia offering ever-green foliage in a range of red and brown shades.

3. Pour the compost into the container until it is three quarters full, ready for placing the plants in their pots onto the compost surface.

4. Place the plants on the compost to check their planting depth. Ideally the rim of their pots will be just below the rim of the pot they are being transplanted into. Experiment with positioning the plants to get the best visual effect. Leave a small gap in between each plant. If there are no gaps at all, lose a plant to make more room, or use a bigger container if you have your heart set on that particular planting combination.

# Feature container recipes

These container recipes celebrate the diversity of the modern cottage garden in a small space. Planting a range of plants in the same container adds a fullness and excitement to the patio, and a selection of mixed containers can make the patio look like a stylish garden in its own right. Lonely, singly planted pots often show off more bare compost than pot, and they struggle to integrate well to make a joined up area of planting. Take some inspiration from these planting combinations to be bold and experiment with plants that can add new life and style to your patio.

**Give spring a fresh, multicoloured start on your patio.** The abundance of a late summer garden can be recreated—in spring—in a large single pot by blending reliable prairie plants with timeless cottage garden classics. The euphorbia presents a kaleidoscope of colour on a single plant, with lime-green flowers, maroon stems, and bronze foliage, which is strawberry red when it shoots in early spring. Two different *Carex* plants add height and movement to the display, and the saxifrage gives the edge of the pot an old-fashioned flourish. The daisy *Bellis perennis* adds a final shot of colour and can be removed after flowering to allow the other plants to fill the pot.

### Plants in the container
*Bellis perennis* Bellissima Series

*Carex buchananii*

*Carex comans* green-leaved

*Erysimum* 'Bowles's Mauve'

*Euphorbia amygdaloides* 'Purpurea'

*Saxifraga* Touran Red

**Fullness and elegance are in short supply at the end of winter, but this pot will buck the trend.**
Here is a container for squeezing into a small space to add some welcome colour at the end of winter. The euphorbia is smaller in stature than the commonly seen *Euphorbia characias* subsp. *wulfenii*, growing to around 75cm (2ft 6in) tall. The saxifrage and anemone provide some fresh flowers and traditional style but still blend well with the carex, which will ensure that the container is bright all year round.

**Plants in the container**

*Anemone blanda*

*Carex oshimensis* 'Eversheen'

*Euphorbia ×martini*

*Saxifraga* 'White Pixie'

**Here is an easy way to add some unusual summer elegance to containers.** Take two classic components—one each from the traditional cottage garden and new perennial styles—and partner them with a contemporary plant of the moment, and you can have a self-contained modern cottage garden in the tiniest of spaces. Asters and achilleas are two heavyweights of the English cottage garden and new perennial styles respectively. A complementary echeveria adds a finishing element of structure and foliage detail. In cold areas, move the echeveria to its own pot before winter so it can be brought indoors and placed on a sunny windowsill until the following summer.

**Plants in the container**

*Achillea millefolium*

*Aster* 'Victoria'

*Echeveria elegans*

**Some unusual container partners join a centre-piece shrub rose.** Roses in containers are a staple of the traditional English garden but they don't flower continuously enough to justify a pot to themselves, especially in a small garden where plants need to work hard. 'Goldsturm' rudbeckia makes a great flowering partner for the end of summer and early fall, while the calibrachoa provides charming flowers all summer long to add some finesse to the display. *Carex oshimensis* Everest has a wonderfully graceful shape, with gently arching stems that hide the bare base of the stems of the rose.

Plant roses in pots so that the bulky part where the stems join the roots is at least 5cm (2in) below the rim of the pot. This will prevent the rose from drying out and will keep it well anchored.

**Plants in the container**

*Calibrachoa* Cabaret Red Improved

*Carex oshimensis* Everest

*Rosa* Vanessa Bell

*Rudbeckia fulgida* var. *sullivantii* 'Goldsturm'

**A container of vigorous plants celebrates the abundance of summer.** Nemesia is a classic cottage garden annual with sprawling stems dripping in cool blossom in summer. It forms the backbone of this container until late summer when the coreopsis majestically rises and shows off its bright blooms, which light up so many borders as the season ends. The calibrachoa is a vigorous spreader, but planting it around the rim of the container allows it to grow out and create a much bigger display than the diameter of the pot alone.

**Plants in the container**

*Calibrachoa* Can-can Terracotta

*Carex oshimensis* Everest

*Coreopsis grandiflora* SunKiss

*Diascia* 'Divara White'

**An easy-to-grow and free-flowering combination creates a classic, contemporary, and uncomplicated container.** *Argyranthemum frutescens* (also known as marguerite) is a plant that bridges the two styles that join together to make a modern cottage garden. Its sturdy stems of daisy flowers and neat habit are at home in both a new perennial border and a cottage garden. It is a fine plant for growing in a container. Chop it back to near ground level in early spring and there is ample space to plant pretty diascias underneath.

**Plants in the container**

*Argyranthemum frutescens*

*Diascia* 'Diamond Pink'

**A drought-tolerant mix makes a year-round hanging basket.** Here is an easy hanging-basket display that features a carpet of low-growing sedums beneath the tall flowering stems of cottage garden favourite catmint, with drought-tolerant rosemary and ivy completing the planting to mix contemporary with classic. The basket was planted with two parts multipurpose compost to one part grit and still looks vibrant during a long, hot summer. The sedums can easily be removed, potted up, and brought undercover in winter in cold areas.

Plant succulents just above the compost surface to prevent the risk of the crowns rotting in wet conditions.

**Plants in the container**

*Hedera helix* 'White Wonder'

*Nepeta grandiflora* 'Summer Magic'

*Rosmarinus officinalis*

*Sedum album* 'Coral Carpet'

*Sedum hispanicum* 'Blue Carpet'

*Sedum tetractinum* 'Coral Reef'

### Add softness to a formal winter container.

Traditional winter containers can be a given a new twist with the addition of soft, silver-leaved brachyglottis and the dramatic, deep-coloured strands of wispy grass *Uncinia rubra*, which isn't winter hardy but can be treated as a bedding plant and grown from a new plant each year.

**Plants in the container**

*Brachyglottis* 'Walberton's Silver Dormouse'

*Polyanthus* hybrid

*Uncinia rubra*

Winter viola

### Celebrate bright and bold autumn colours.

The beginning of autumn is among the most colourful times of year, and containers packed with plants in full flower ensure that the passing of summer doesn't signal the end of the garden looking interesting for the year. Rudbeckias are star plants for early autumn and 'Little Goldstar' is handy for small spaces, growing and spreading to just 50cm (1ft 8in). Hardy chrysanthemums are star plants of the cottage garden and provide colour until the frosts, while an evergreen grass will provide some contrast and soften the edge of the pot.

**Plants in the container**

*Carex oshimensis* 'Eversheen'

Hardy chrysanthemum

*Rudbeckia fulgida* 'Little Goldstar'

# A Touch of the Exotic: Succulents in the Modern Cottage Garden

Succulents have been capturing the imagination of plant lovers, but they are often grown indoors in isolation or in a homogeneous group. Planted alongside perennials and shrubs in a modern cottage garden, however, succulents can bring an extra twist to the idea of fusion. Most are not hardy but if added to the garden after the risk of frost has passed, they can then be removed and potted up to spend the late autumn, winter, and spring indoors as houseplants.

The best impact will come from planting succulents together in containers, where the contrast of textures and colours can be concentrated in one area. Most succulents are too small to make an impact in a garden border even if the soil conditions and aspect are right, but they become prominent plants when added to pots and even to hanging baskets. This allows the intricate forms and details of sempervivums, echeverias, aeoniums, and sedums to be appreciated at close hand.

Succulent *Peper-omia graveolens* 'Ruby Glow' and *Calibrachoa* Can-can Terracotta make perfect part-ners for a summer container display that is a mix of the traditional and the contemporary.

The key with this fusion of styles is to highlight what most succulent plants thrive on: warmth, free-drainage, and sunny, dry conditions. There are many cottage garden plants and newly popular perennials that like the same conditions.

Catmint, such as the short-growing *Nepeta grandiflora* 'Summer Magic', is one of these perennials: its greyish-green leaves blend superbly with similarly coloured succulents such as *Sedum hispanicum* 'Blue Carpet', which makes a neat, trailing mat of greyish-blue growth.

Try mixing and matching succulents with other drought-tolerant, sun-loving plants such as eryngiums, dwarf lavenders such as 'Hidcote' and 'Munstead', and varieties of perennial wallflowers such as *Erysimum* 'Bowles's Mauve', which flowers in spring and blooms all summer and into autumn. Also try them with Mediterranean herbs such as matt-forming oregano. For a dry prairie feeling, grow trailing sedums or echeverias beneath the wispy strands of *Pennisetum orientale* and the sword-like leaves of *Libertia peregrinans*.

# A Year
# in the
# Modern
# Cottage
# Garden

## Growing and Looking
## After the Garden
## Season by Season

The modern cottage garden is a feast
of colour, texture, and excitement in
every season.

So how can the modern cottage garden style be achieved and kept looking its best year round, and for the longer term?

A good place to start is to look at the classic components through the seasons and to see which plants from the contributing styles you can grow together in each season.

The reality is that most of us end up with a garden that looks considerably better in the summer than it does at any other time. While this is understandable and even part of the rhythm of nature, some simple plant choices and combinations will stretch the season so that you will want to photograph and sit in the garden for longer than just high summer.

A host of spring-flowering perennials, bulbs, and early-flowering shrubs can blend together to make the garden feel full and vibrant at a time when many perennials and grasses are only just emerging from their winter dormancy. Choosing a good mix of plants that flower from early summer until the first frosts of winter will also ensure that the garden looks good for longer periods. And finally evergreen grasses, perennial seedheads, and monochrome skeletons of deciduous grasses will greatly enhance the look of a garden that was once traditional and bare in winter.

The starting point for my garden was identifying the evergreen plants that would form the backbone—in other words, the plants that I could depend on to look good and noticeable all year round. Then everything else could be planted around them.

I aimed for at least a third of the garden (including areas of containers) to be evergreen, mostly in the form of shrubs such as hebes, euonymus, and ivies, grasses such as *Carex* and *Stipa* varieties, and also perennial evergreen *Erysimum* 'Bowles's Mauve'. The rest of the garden is a mix of flowering perennials and roses, with summer-flowering annuals providing the finishing touch.

Planning and planting the tallest plants first and then moving on to shorter plants before the lowest edging plants is a good way of narrowing down the plant selections if you are not sure where to start in creating a modern cottage garden.

Then, before you know it, the question becomes how to keep the garden looking its best. What to do with a plant, and when, seems to cause many gardeners unnecessary worry. Should I have pruned that plant? Did I feed it often enough? How can I make it grow quicker? I know from experience that there can be a fear that if a plant isn't pruned at the right time, or planted in exactly the right place, then it will all of a sudden give up the ghost and die. Yet very few of the jobs recommended to gardeners are life and death matters. With this in mind, see the seasonal gardening tasks that I outline in this part of the book, not as an emergency list of things that have to be done to save your garden, but rather as tasks that will help make sure that your garden looks as healthy, vibrant, and flower-packed as possible, and that the plants in it look good for the maximum amount of time. That's certainly something that every gardener will welcome.

# Spring

Spring is surely the most joyous season in the garden. Seeing signs of life in a place that seemed frozen in time only weeks before unsurprisingly puts a spring in the gardener's step. The garden changes more in a single day than it will in any other season. Go away for a week in spring and the garden can be almost unrecognizable when you get back. Like a friend who quits their job to go travelling and comes back a different person, so the garden can go through such a big transformation in a very short period of time that you begin to wonder if you really know it at all.

In spring, delights can be found in so many places in the garden. Although the peak season of many perennials and shrubs is some way off, the attentive gardener will discover unheralded beauty. Even small signs of life—the first appearance above ground of a treasured hardy geranium or the sprouting of ghostly white new shoots of eventually silver sparkling brunnera leaves—become a source of fascination and excitement. They stand out against the leaves that have limped through winter on evergreen shrubs, telling a story of hope and expectation.

To transform your garden in spring, start by trying to make sure that it doesn't rely on one or two plants to provide all the colour and the talking points. If they fail, the garden can look bare and monotonous. For all the beauty of tulips and daffodils, they needn't be "get out of jail" plants that provide all the season's colour. Along with early-flowering shrubs and perennials, add a mix of plants with intriguing, multicoloured leaves and the garden can look whole in spring, rather than a place with a few

The garden is never fresher than when plants have emerged into full leaf and flower in spring.

sporadic highlights of colour provided by pockets of daffodils, primroses, or tulips.

Despite the light show of autumn, for me, foliage is never more beautiful than in spring, when new leaves shimmer in the low sun and the vivid colours of youthful vigour give the garden a special glow. The existence of the leaf at all is enough to get excited about. Fresh foliage—of a new shoot on a rose or a spotty leaved pulmonaria—is the much-undervalued, true herald of spring in the garden.

Many plants are worth growing for their spring leaves alone, to make the modern cottage garden a riot of foliage hues that challenges even the finest of autumn colours. Combined with some surprisingly understated flowering plants that always seem to miss the limelight, this season can be about a rich

tapestry of colours as well as the obviously bright and cheerful displays of early-flowering bulbs that are so often relied upon in this season.

Euphorbias provide a diverse mixture of spring colours and shout them loud and proud through their finger-like foliage and intricate but also bold and unmissable flowerheads. The leaves of *Euphorbia amygdaloides* 'Purpurea' are flushed with a mix of burnt red and maroon, while *Euphorbia characias* subsp. *wulfenii* produces leaves in a muted mix of green and almost powder blue beneath their frothy lime-green flowerheads.

Equally as multicoloured is *Spiraea japonica* 'Goldflame', a plant that is most easily recognized by its luminous lime-green leaves and flat purple flowers. But its most intriguing and sophisticated display of colour comes in early spring as the leaves start to form. They carry a range of reddish shades as they start to develop, with the gradations of colour on such small shoots providing one of the first real get-up-close-and-have-a-look moments of spring.

*Abelia grandiflora* has similarly exquisite spring leaves that will glow in the sunshine and show off their own muted spectrum of orange, bronze, and red. The show will be long forgotten by the time that its flowers appear in late summer, but in the moment of spring it is a work of art to be appreciated like a painting that is in a gallery for a limited period, only to be whisked away just when it was becoming familiar. The old adage attributed to circus promoter P. T. Barnum, "Always leave them wanting more," is the brief that all plants seem to have been given in spring. That's all part of the excitement. If we had steak and fries to eat every night, I expect we'd soon get bored of it.

Roses can add tremendous colour to the garden in spring through their soft young shoots, many of which will show no trace of the sharp spines that will follow later. The rose called Lady Emma Hamilton produces gorgeously colour-toned stems before its rich orangey bronze blooms appear, with new leaves bearing a delightful mix of bronze, purple, and rusty red shades. It is a tremendous partner for purple-flowered tulips or brown or rust-coloured evergreen grasses.

Other roses with beautiful new shoots in spring include Munstead Wood which develops bronze-red shoots before its highly scented, purple ruffled flowers, and climbing rose Mortimer Sackler which will provide red hues through its young leaves before it produces sprays of rose-pink semi-double flowers.

The new perennial planting style isn't noted for its spring show, but to provide depth and character to the arrival of a new season in the garden, plenty of plants from the style can be added to eye-catching cottage garden plants that save their best for spring. Evergreen grasses play a vital role in keeping the garden looking full and lush at a time when there can easily be a lot of bare gaps.

**Opposite:** The glorious leaves and flowerheads of *Euphorbia characias* subsp. *wulfenii* are bold and unmissable in the garden at the start of spring.

**Right:** The fresh, glossy new growth of a Lady Emma Hamilton rose gives the garden a special spring glow.

*Carex buchananii* adds height and muted bronze colouring to contrast with fresh spring colours.

Upright bronze-leaved *Carex buchananii* provides welcome height as well as bronze colouring in spring and *C. buchananii* 'Red Rooster' produces more maroon shades, its strands of foliage tipped with intriguing rolled-up ends. Tremendous plants for adding a modern twist to a spring container, they also make a fine backdrop for orange or dark purple tulips.

Helping banish the amount of brown soil on show in spring is evergreen sedge *Carex oshimensis* 'Evergold', which produces wide clumps of green-and-cream variegated leaves that will form a fine spring show if spring-flowering bulbs are scattered around them. The old leaves will have a yellowish-brown edge, which brings a strangely autumnal slant to a show of vibrant spring flowers.

The leaves of *Sanguisorba officinalis* 'Red Thunder' will add an edge to the spring garden too—literally—with their jagged leaves that look as if they have been trimmed with pinking shears. Plant it close to the front of a border or a large container so the leaves aren't missed because they are a true work of natural art. Later in summer their burgundy-red capsule-shaped flowers will steal the show and then also add form to the garden in winter.

Another potentially tricky time to ensure that there is a wide range of colours in the garden is in the transition between spring and summer. Many dependable flowering plants such as tulips, pulmonarias, and spring anemones (*Anemone nemorosa*) will fade, and some will start showing tired-looking foliage too. Pulmonarias and also hardy geraniums that finish flowering in early summer can be chopped back to ground level with garden shears when they create gaps in the garden.

This is where a group of plants that were once a backbone of an English country garden can come to the fore: hardy annuals. Blend them with the rapidly developing foliage of prairie perennials, evergreen grasses, and sedges, and they will help knit the border together.

## SPRING-FLOWERING PERENNIALS

Many perennial plants that look good in spring produce their best display in a shady, or at least partially shady, part of the garden. Among iconic cottage garden perennials for shade is bleeding heart, *Lamprocapnos spectabilis* (which most gardeners have long known as *Dicentra spectabilis*, but tradition isn't enough to stop the experts from renaming it). A nimble plant, it is happy to find its way among shrubs and grasses to produce its classic dangling flower stems at the end of spring. As well as the traditional pink flower there is also a classy white form, 'Alba'. Keep its roots damp and shaded and it can flower well in full sun too.

*Pulmonaria* is the one shade-tolerant plant that you can guarantee will be in flower at Easter, regardless of when Easter falls. If Easter is

early, then this perennial will be a star of the moment, among the first perennials to flower. If Easter is later, then it will still be in bloom and the foliage often has distinctive spotting, which adds extra detail to the spring garden. A somewhat ghostly presence, it will disappear into the background once the first roses of the summer flower, its low-lying leaves getting lost among summer's abundant growth, but if you cut it back, it can produce a fresh new flush of leaves. Think of them as a famous actor in between movies. You forget about them for a few months and then suddenly they are everywhere again. Be rest assured, in the following year your pulmonaria will return and delight you (and the bees) all over again. Most are blue-flowered, but there are also white forms such as 'Sissinghurst White', while *Pulmonaria rubra* is a delightful soft red.

Another cottage garden classic that is cut from the same cloth (well, in the same plant family anyway) is *Brunnera macrophylla* 'Jack Frost' which has leaves with a wonderful silvery patterning and airy blue flowers at the same time as *Pulmonaria*. Both look effective when planted in big clumps, but a single plant in a container will also look fresh and interesting, and both work well among spring bulbs. It is a slug magnet, though, so take precautions.

The gentle development of *Saxifraga* Touran Red is a joy to watch in spring. Its transition from producing a display of initial perky, upright flower stems in early spring to a cascade of flowers that gracefully tumble over the edge of a container or border is an attractive reminder that the growing season is developing. The flowers also age gracefully, slowly losing their rich magenta colour but replacing it with a bleached pastel pink.

**Above left:** *Lamprocapnos spectabilis* 'Alba' is a superb plant for weaving in among shrubs and grasses to add extra interest in spring.

**Below:** The delicate but cold-tolerant flowers of *Pulmonaria rubra* add a pretty flourish to the garden in early spring.

Lily of the valley (*Convallaria majalis*) is an all-time classic spring garden flower with that prized spring asset: a sweet and delicious scent. It grows best in a damp and shady corner where it will spread as much as you let it. Despite the undoubted beauty and scent of the flowers, it is not the most beautiful of plants so try mixing it with the beautiful damp-loving grass *Acorus gramineus* 'Ogon', which has gently leaning yellowy gold variegated leaves, or broad-leaved *Hakonechloa macra* which will grow in damp soil and semi-shade.

## SPRING BEDDING PLANTS

Growing spring bedding plants among bulbs has for too long been considered the preserve of community parks and municipal gardens. These plants can really give the garden an extra lift in the season, especially in containers and small spaces, and their bright colours stand out beautifully if framed by wispy grasses. Brightly coloured bedding daisies (*Bellis perennis*) mingle wonderfully with evergreen grasses, their perky flower stalks injecting some brash colour to a more sophisticated background. They are thirsty plants, preferring a damp soil and needing regular attention in pots in a dry spring, but they are worth it because the flowering show will go on for weeks.

Also try violas, another bedding classic, to provide some crisp, neat colour to the garden in late winter and spring. They can keep flowering until summer. Plant them around the edges of containers of grasses and evergreen shrubs where the sharpness of their flowers will stand out strongly.

Wallflowers will bring a more complex show of colours to the modern cottage garden in spring, and their blooms always tug at the heart strings. These are truly the cottage garden plants of bygone days, when plant choice was limited and gardeners would grow most of their garden flowers from seed, sowing in summer for flowers the following year, with not an impulse garden centre buy in sight. Dry, stony soil that gets baked by sun is crying out to be planted with wallflowers in autumn for

**Above left:** Bedding daisies add sharp and vibrant colour in spring and can add the finishing touch to a border edge or mixed container.

**Left:** Perennial wallflower *Erysimum* 'Apricot Twist' adds warm shades to the garden at the end of spring and through summer and combines effectively with brown and red foliage.

a wonderful show in the following spring. Plant them among evergreen shrubs and grasses and around low-growing spring-flowering perennials such as hardy *Pulmonaria* 'Trevi Fountain'. Perennials such as *Erysimum* 'Bowles's Mauve' and 'Apricot Twist' will start flowering a bit later at the end of spring but will keep flowering all summer and into autumn, as well as remaining evergreen.

Spring bulbs are often the first flowers of the year to make an impact in the garden, but despite their uplifting presence in isolation, they have more impact when planted with others. To get the best from spring bulbs, plant them in groups among established backbone plants such as evergreen shrubs and grasses or among plants that have colourful foliage in spring. Plant at least five of each type of bulb in spaces through borders and beds to give pockets of vivid colour in spring.

# CARING FOR THE GARDEN IN SPRING

This is the season when enthusiasm and eagerness are the energy behind each gardening task. The joy of seeing plants burst into life is paired with the excitement of knowing that each plant added and divided and each seed sown can bring bright, bold, and memorable results, some of which can last for years. This is the season where the garden changes so much that there is something new to see—and do—every day.

## To-do list for spring

☐ Protect the new shoots of perennials from slugs and snails.

☐ Lift and divide herbaceous perennials that have formed large plants.

☐ Grow new perennials in pots until you have large enough plants to add to the garden.

☐ Remove perennial weeds from the centre of shrubs and roses before the unwanted plants are hidden from view.

Tease the roots apart on pot-bound plants that you are going to plant, to help them explore the new soil.

**Above left:** Top-dress the compost surface of container plants after rain to hold in moisture and make them look neat.

**Above:** Plant climbers at an angle towards the wall or fence you want it to grow up.

☐ Mulch roses and shrubs and any plants requiring a damp, moisture retentive soil in order to thrive.

☐ Feed roses and other summer-flowering shrubs with a balanced granular fertilizer.

☐ Plant up hanging baskets at the end of spring and move them undercover on cold nights if they contain frost-tender plants.

☐ Remove and replace the top 5cm (2in) of compost from containers that are housing permanent plants.

When you plant containerized roses, make sure that the bulky part where the stems join the roots sits at least 5cm (2in) below soil level.

Thinly sow hardy annuals such as calendulas directly into a patch of well-raked soil in full sun and seeds should germinate in two or three weeks.

Deadhead spring-flowering plants such as bellis and dianthus to keep the display of flowers looking sharp. Pinch them out by hand to avoid damaging fresh flowers.

Stake herbaceous perennials, especially those that will grow very tall such as Aster 'Kylie' (pictured).

## DIVISION

Lifting a large plant, breaking it up into smaller plants, and planting them through the garden is handy if you want to create rhythm in the garden by repeat planting. Only divide old plants (at least three years old) and only divide plants that you are sure you want more of. Some plants end up being plastered all over a garden simply because they are easy to divide, and although this may be cost effective, it can make the garden look very same-y and only full-looking when that particular plant is looking good. Perennial plants will need dividing once they have been in the same spot for three or four years or they can lose their vigour and flower poorly.

If your soil is light, then lifting and dividing the plants with a fork and then breaking the clump into pieces with your hands or a hand trowel should prove sufficient. Only resort to placing two forks back to back into the plant for large, congested clumps that are very difficult to prize apart. Resist the temptation to split a clump into too many pieces because ten tiny plants will have less impact than one substantial plant. Small divisions may not flower in the first year either.

## DEALING WITH SLUGS

It's not just death and taxes that are inevitable. A lot of frustrated gardeners would add slugs to this saying too. The list of remedies, chemicals, and barriers that are used to stop slugs is the stuff of legend and a book on its own. But there is one action you can take that will heavily stack the odds in your favour when it comes to getting the better of slugs and that is nematodes. These are microscopic parasites that are watered into the soil when soil temperatures are above 5°C (41°F). The next best trick is that whatever you plant, be it perennials or hardened off, half-hardy annuals raised from seed, make sure they are good-sized plants before you plant them in the garden. The bigger the plant, the more likely it is to be able to shrug off a slug attack.

Plants particularly at risk from slugs include brunnera, erigerons, heleniums, honeywort (*Cerinthe*), hostas, and Shasta daisies (*Leucanthemum*). The plants that I would call slug-proof from experience are carex, erysimums, euphorbias, hardy geraniums, ivies, and roses.

# Summer

In places where summer is the only season of the year, we might grow tired of the abundance of sights, scents, and sounds that make it so special. Still, it would be nice to find out if that would be the case. Even as it is, this is the season of indulgence. Long days allow the garden to be explored and enjoyed for hours, and plants change daily, a new film playing each day to a captivated audience, the gardener seeing the results that have long been waited for.

The most spectacular areas of planting in the garden in summer never rely on one plant to grab all the attention (and let's be honest, we all find attention seekers unbearable after a while). Repeat planting—including the same plant along a stretch of border or throughout a garden—is often recommended and has its merits in helping make an area look joined up. But if the trick is played too many times, then the garden can lack diversity and intrigue. And in a small space, it is all very well being told to plant in fives or sevens, but this severely limits how many different plants you can grow, as if being limited in the number of plants you could grow wasn't frustrating enough already.

Wholesale repeat planting is mainly the preserve of the gardener with acres at their disposal, although it can work with summer-flowering bulbs such as alliums, which are easy to squeeze into gaps in a border to add bright colour and structure that can last all year if the seedheads are left intact on the plant. Plant them among plants with airy flowers such as heucheras, and the flowers will look like they are suspended in mid-air.

Summer is the time of abundance and fullness, when the garden is rich with plants that have reached maturity and, for many, their flowering peak. Alliums are useful for repeat-planting in a small space among grasses and other perennials, popping up in between them to add splashes of extra colour.

When space is limited, it is far better to stick to occasionally repeating evergreen shrubs (but it doesn't have to be the same ones), which will form a backbone for the garden. Although they will go almost unnoticed in summer, they will be worth their weight in gold in winter for providing colour and form to complement dormant perennials.

Rather than repeating lots of the same flowering plant, try growing different varieties of it if you hit on a plant that grows well in your garden or that you are fond of. This leaves room for the discovery of the assets of new plants and increases the diversity of fragrances, leaf colours, and flower forms in the garden, without its becoming a random collection of plant oddities.

## SUMMER BEDDING PLANTS

If ever a group of plants gets a bad press, it's bedding plants that flower in summer. Maybe it's because they are considered too brash and gaudy and only a short-term solution because of the need to replace them every year. Yet the same could be said of tulips (they are rarely as good in their second year as in their first), and these are still much-championed plants.

The real shame about summer bedding plants is that they are so often grown en masse in big clumps and often surrounded by bare soil or identical plants for much of the year. And yet some of them can greatly enhance a mixed display of plants that combines shrubs, flowering perennials, and grasses if they are used not sparingly but selectively. Growing summer bedding with other plants is like only eating bananas on their own and then one day discovering how good they taste alongside pancakes and maple syrup.

Summer bedding plants can be priceless in the modern cottage garden, and no plant snob who turns their nose up at them can convince me otherwise. Perhaps the one that lends itself to the style the most is *Calibrachoa*. It is related to petunias and is an elegant plant that is more slender and slim—both in flowers and leaves—than petunias but more tolerant of drought and less likely to run riot and need cutting back. The orange forms Can-can Coral Reef (light orange with a hint of salmon pink) and Can-can Terracotta (orange and yellow with a mottled effect) are a perfect fit for the modern cottage garden because they complement

**Above:** Calibrachoas gently tumble over the edges of containers without becoming too dominant and choking surrounding plants.

**Right:** Neat and compact *Diascia* 'Diamond Pink' will produce clouds of blossom beneath tall plants in containers or at border edges.

many rust-coloured grasses such as orange-brown *Carex testacea* or brown *Carex buchananii.*

Calibrachoas also have an old-fashioned charm in the way they gently meander around the edges of borders or containers and evoke a memory of hanging baskets edged with petunias in years gone by. Or grow a trailing *Bidens* species, dainty plants with flowers that resemble those of coreopsis, to add some elegant, sunny yellow blossom to the edges of paths or pots through summer and autumn.

Nemesias and diascias will flower through until the first frosts and may also scrape through winter if grown in soil or compost that drains exceptionally well. Their delicate pastel-coloured flowers are pure old-fashioned charm in a small but perfectly formed package. Most don't grow more than 30cm (1ft) tall. Try a 'Diamond Pink' diascia below a pink echinacea to create two tiers of complementary colour.

Pelargoniums have a lot to offer the garden, and among the finest is 'Lady Plymouth' with its lemon-scented, palest green, variegated leaves and delicate pink flowers. It will add elegance to a container or sunny border where the soil drains well. Try planting one in a container with *Stipa tenuissima* and placing it near a pink or salmon shrub rose for some summer sophistication. Pot it up and bring it indoors before winter and it will make a fine houseplant on a well-lit windowsill.

Brasher, but also a gift to the gardener creating a mixed border, are African marigolds. So often grown in isolation where their pompon heads provide a mass of summer colour, they take on a new, subtler lease of life when mixed with perennial rudbeckias and bronze grasses such as *Uncinia rubra.*

## SUMMER-FLOWERING SHRUBS

Shrubs are the mainstay of many a garden, but they often end up being plants that we tolerate rather than enjoy. They can become too big for their boots, demanding more space than their merits warrant. And if a shrub gets too big it can lack vigour and therefore not flower as well as it would have if it was regularly pruned. Some shrubs—such as lilacs—also have a short flowering period and don't justify the space they take up, especially if the garden is small. Focus on shrubs that flower all summer to increase the chances that they will mingle well with other plants to create exciting combinations of texture and colour.

An old-fashioned classic that will bring tiers of colour to the border all summer is the hardy fuchsia. These plants are undervalued for their ability to mingle with other plants and form graceful, attractive shapes, sometimes clothed in eye-catching variegated foliage. Perhaps hardy fuchsias are ignored because so many tender fuchsias wither in the winter and are brash and unsubtle, but few shrubs are as easy to grow and as long-flowering as hardy fuchsias. Some are elegant, too, especially varieties of *Fuchsia magellanica*. 'Thompsonii' is a particularly fine form, with slim hot pink flowers and stems in a slightly more muted shade of pink. Their gracefully arching stems are perfect for hanging over flatter plants.

Varieties of *Fuchsia magellanica* add graceful flowers to the garden in summer and autumn.

*Salvia* 'Hot Lips' makes a bushy but slender shrub that will flower all through summer and fall in a sunny, well-drained part of the garden.

Also try the reliable *Sedum* 'Autumn Joy' which produces domes of maroon or pink flowers on flat flowerheads that will create a raised floor of colour when the fuchsia is still in full bloom.

*Hydrangea arborescens* 'Annabelle' is a real hard-working shrub, producing incredible balls of blossom from early summer to early autumn, with blooms from the top to the bottom of the plant. It is a real gift to a semi-shaded part of the garden. The flowers transform from zingy green to pure white to keep the garden feeling fresh. Try underplanting it with a spreading grass such as *Hakonechloa macra* and the combination will provide structure into autumn and winter too.

For a shrub full of old-fashioned charm consider shrubby salvias if your soil drains well and is sheltered. These plants couldn't be further away from bedding salvias in looks, with dainty, lipped flowers in pastel pink shades, white, and red. They flower from early summer until the first frosts; red and white 'Hot Lips' is perhaps the best known, but the slightly more subtle 'Pink Blush' will perfectly complement hollyhocks and foxgloves.

## ANNUALS FROM SEED

These plants are incredibly undervalued and seldom given the spotlight, but they are tremendous additions to the modern cottage garden. Hardy annuals are especially valuable in making a new border look full in its first year. A couple of generations ago, before you could drive to a garden centre and pick up an array of perky, ready-to-plant perennials in plastic pots, hardy annuals were more widely grown, but in a convenience-obsessed age, it is only really sweet peas—sold as potted plants—that have retained their popularity in this group.

The luxury of being able to sow hardy annuals direct onto border soil in autumn or early spring and to have plants that flower in early summer used to be a massive asset in making a full and colourful garden, and it

still should be today. Although we have a world of choice at our fingertips now, hardy annuals are true garden classics that deserve to mix with the more popular perennials of the twenty-first century.

Many hardy annuals such as stock (*Matthiola incana*), linaria, and cornflower (*Centaurea cyanus*) would have been essential components of a traditional cottage garden, but their reliance on being grown from seed has undoubtedly halted any wider appeal. Yet a whole world of new planting combinations can be explored if you mix them with other plants. Now is the time for them to take the spotlight once more because they are not difficult to grow from seed and can complement foliage perennials with an intriguing palette of colours in early summer. The most famous and never-out-of-fashion hardy annual is of course the sweet pea.

The easiest way to blend these delightful flowers into a mixed border is to insert bamboo cane wigwams or obelisks into the soil in early spring and plant young sweet peas at the base of them. Young plants will need protection from slugs, but the bigger the plant, the less at risk of slug attack it will be. Sweet peas produce their best results when grown in deep, rich soil. Remember to check the base of the plants regularly during summer and if the soil is dry, soak them thoroughly until puddles form at the base of the plant. This will help prevent the plants from getting mildew, which turns healthy green leaves to tired old grey ones.

**Above left:** Hardy annuals can be sown directly into the garden soil in early spring and they will flower in the same summer, proving very useful for providing colour to a new garden.

**Above right:** Sowing seed of hardy annuals such as night-scented stock directly into the border is a cheap and effective way to fill gaps.

For colour lower down, pot marigolds (*Calendula* varieties) are priceless for their longevity of flowering: 'Princess Orange Black' bears flowers on 50cm (1ft 8in) stems that make as strong an impact in a border in summer as the most established of perennials, provided the flowers are promptly snipped off as their petals fall.

To cover ground in the first year, nasturtiums will prove very valuable. These plants have a reputation—and rightly so in many cases—of spreading like wildfire, but be selective with the varieties that you grow and they are a tremendously useful plant for covering ground and edging containers. 'Jewel Mix' is a variety that knows its place, growing to around 30cm (1ft) wide and tall. The seeds are large and easy to sow. Just push one into a suitably sized gap in any sunny part of the garden, so long as the soil drains reasonably well. Try sowing it around the plants that you know will have the most flowering impact in a young border, and it will bridge the gaps between different flowering plants with its rounded foliage and simple hot-coloured flowers.

One of the strangest-looking hardy annuals but surely among the most beautiful is *Cerinthe major* 'Purpurascens'. With its thick glaucous leaves and the gorgeous blends of blue, bronze, and green on its flowering shoot tips, it looks like a far more permanent presence in the garden than an annual. It adds rich, full-bodied colour to the front of a border, making sure that interest doesn't peter out along the edges.

**Right:** Pot marigolds add both brightness and warmth to the garden all through summer if swiftly deadheaded as the flowers fade.

**Far right:** *Cerinthe major* 'Purpurascens' flowers in summer after being sown in spring yet manages to look like it is a permanent border fixture.

As well as being practical plants in terms of helping fill space and being easy to grow, other hardy annuals will become star plants in their own right and not just background players. Night-scented stocks (*Matthiola longipetala*) fall into this category. The sweet scent of their flowers is released into the air in the evening as if the plant was getting ready to go out to the theatre. Sow them by border edges and near seating areas in the garden so that the scent can be savoured.

Half-hardy annuals can't be sown directly onto the soil until the risk of frost has gone, but if you sow them indoors, pot them up, and leave them outside during the day in spring to acclimatize to the great outdoors, you can have some sizeable plants for the garden at the end of spring.

Cosmos is a classic, its airy, simple, pastel-coloured flowers working well in the shelter of tall perennials such as *Eutrochium maculatum* (Joe Pye weed or *Eupatorium maculatum*). With its loose, light, feathery foliage, cosmos seemingly ghosts into a border and manages to produce a sizeable plant without taking up much visible space. It works wonderfully well among similarly slender perennials such as *Perovskia* 'Blue Spire'.

Many cosmos are greedy plants that will do their best to hog attention. Grown in light soil and full sun, they can become a billowing mass of frothy leaves and saucer-shaped flowers. Plant them around some permanent fixtures in the border—a young tree, evergreen shrubs, or plants with contrasting foliage—to break up the display and hide gaps between plants.

Half-hardy annuals can also add scent to the garden if you grow tobacco plant (*Nicotiana sylvestris*). A tall plant with unusual flowerheads that resemble tassel lampshades, it can be leggy but is perfect for weaving through a tall perennial such as powder-blue *Campanula lactiflora* or through a tall grass such as *Calamagrostis brachytricha*.

**Opposite:** *Cosmos* 'Versailles Tetra' finds a perfect partner in the silvery blue flowers and stems of *Perovskia* 'Blue Spire' and it also gels well with taller perennials that can help support it, such as *Eutrochium maculatum* behind it.

**Right:** Cosmos such as 'Antiquity' will add a significant floral display to the garden in summer and blend well with late-flowering perennials at the end of the season.

*Cleome* varieties are also tall half-hardy annuals that mix well with perennials. These statuesque plants produce their spidery blooms in shades of pink, white, and pale purple and flower until the frosts, when their flowerheads will add to the winter structure of the garden. Just be careful not to get too close to the sharp spines on the stems.

For some rich, warm colours to add depth to a border in summer, annual rudbeckias bring a wider mix of colours than the perennial ones provide, with the strawberry-red flowers of 'Cherry Brandy' or the two-tone, red and orange 'Cherokee Sunset'. They tend to be short plants, so mixing them with perennial rudbeckias can create two tiers of warm colour in a border or container.

**Left:** After a spring sowing *Cleome hassleriana* 'Helen Campbell' grows quickly to form a statuesque plant by summer when it is tall enough to mix with sizeable border shrubs.

**Below:** Repeat-flowering shrub rose Dame Judi Dench shows gorgeous, rain-resistant, scented flowers through summer and into autumn.

## ROSES

Growing roses is strangely still something of a love-it-or-hate-it subject among gardeners. Some dismiss them as old hat or suggest that they are just twigs for six months. Yet others would happily lose all else from the garden if just the roses could be kept.

The truth is that roses would be considered in a lot more gardens if they were sold as summer-flowering shrubs instead of roses. Some gardeners have a bit of a mental block about growing them. They are worried about diseases such as blackspot and mildew, and that the plants won't look good in the garden for very much of the year. None of this has to be true.

Free-flowering
shrub roses such as
hot pink Gertrude
Jekyll make good
minglers in a border.

Many roses will bloom on and off for six months, and they are also an invaluable plant in spring. Those with intriguingly coloured stems and leaves make a fine accompaniment for many spring-flowering bulbs, and they can hold their own in a mixed container as a backbone plant with their foliage alone if mingled with shorter spring-flowering plants such as bellis and pulmonarias. Then there is the possibility of colourful and attractive hips in autumn and winter.

Roses mingle well with grasses, and the old cliché about roses being lovers of clay soil doesn't mean that they can't be grown with a lot of the prairie perennials that prefer free-draining conditions. It is just a case of being selective with the roses that you grow because there is amazing versatility. *Rosa ×odorata* 'Mutabilis' has so much to offer the modern cottage garden. It grows vigorously in a sandy soil, and flowers from late spring through to the first frosts. Although this tea rose is not completely hardy, shelter and sharp drainage in winter should see it through, and it will tolerate being dug up and potted if you want to be extra careful that it doesn't succumb to the ravages of frost.

A problem can occur in the first year after a rose is planted: the stems become floppy and get bent down to ground level because of the weight of the blooms. This is most common on frilly, double-flowered roses with flowers made up of many petals. The best way to avoid the issue is to not overfeed roses when they are young. If the soil has been enriched with good-quality, well-decayed compost or farmyard manure, then this will be enough to get the roses established until early summer. Then a granular rose food can be sprinkled at the base of each rose and watered into the soil. This food will help the plants produce a good-quality second flush of flowers before autumn arrives.

With the possibility that they will produce bare legs, roses are a natural choice to be border minglers. The old-fashioned idea that roses should be grown in large groups with no other plants highlights all of a rose's bad points. Diseases and pests spread quickly from plant to plant, gaps in flowering leave big lulls in summer, and the winter scene has all the warmth of a graveyard.

Paired with other perennials though, roses are able to thrive, like a school pupil empowered by an encouraging teacher. Grow them with perennials that show good structure into autumn and winter such as *Veronicastrum virginicum* to extend the season of interest in a border. Astrantias, hardy geraniums, and kniphofia all thrive in the clay soil beloved of roses, and the classic partner is *Alchemilla mollis*, which produces its fresh, frothy, yellow-green flowers at the same time as most shrub roses start to bloom. *Alchemilla mollis* can make a tall plant and obscure the flowers of some shorter roses, but *A. epipsila* is a shorter form that will prevent this problem. Good partners for roses also include rudbeckias, which flower well on heavier soils, and their late flowering should coincide with the second or third flush of many repeat-flowering roses.

## CLIMBERS

The abundance of summer is exaggerated if climbers clothe the boundaries of the garden, and many cherished summer plants are those that climb. Make effective use of the boundaries of the garden by growing climbers together, just like plants are grown together in a border. The overall look of a garden can be spoiled by bare, unsightly walls that end

Shrub rose 'Princess Anne' produces scented blooms well into autumn and combines well with the upright flower stems of *Veronicastrum virginicum*, which will look good into winter to provide form and structure once the colour is gone.

Common honey-
suckle (*Lonicera
periclymenum*) is
a vigorous climber
but makes a
beautiful, scented
summer feature if
kept well pruned.

up standing out more than even the loudest of plants. Clothing them with
a combination of climbers will tie a modern cottage garden together
as a whole, softening hard edges and blurring boundaries. An abundance
of climbers with white flowers will also light up a garden's boundaries
as dusk falls, creating an atmospheric and spectacular space on moonlit
summer evenings.

Common honeysuckle (*Lonicera periclymenum*) is vigorous but worth
its weight in gold for its summer scent. The stems twine counter-clockwise,
so plant it to cover a space from right to left. If you want it to cover a wall
behind a bench without much persuasion, plant it on the right-hand side
of the bench and it will naturally grow towards the left-hand side.

Climbing roses are often not done justice in the garden. Allowing them
to grow vertically might seem the right thing to do for a climber, but a
better display of flowers is produced if the stems are stretched out horizontally—which encourages more flowering shoots to develop—and tied
to a support to create a fan shape. Choose the new healthy varieties that
look old-fashioned because there is no hiding place for diseased roses
when they are grown against a wall or trellis. Avoid the frequently recommended 'Zéphirine Drouhin' because it tends to be unhealthy, especially
prone to powdery mildew. Instead, try the gently nodding, pale pink

flowers of the healthier climbing rose The Generous Gardener which will clothe a wall or building up to 4m (13ft) tall. Or for another healthy variety with a strong fragrance and a similar height, 'Compassion' has highly perfumed flowers in salmon-pink with a hint of orangey yellow.

Don't underestimate ivy if you feel that your garden is lacking in old-fashioned charm. Letting ivy climb or trail within reason can help create a relaxed feel in the garden and prevent it from looking too deliberate. It is also a plant that looks healthy and vigorous all year round. Planting ivy doesn't have to mean planting a monster that consumes all that dares cross its path. Try the short-growing variety *Hedera helix* 'Ivalace' which only climbs to a meter tall and also has unusual curled edges to its glossy leaves, which are pointier than the leaves of common ivy.

If the thought of ivy alone for covering a wall in shade sounds limiting, team it with *Clematis* 'Alba Luxurians', which is also a quick grower and a lover of shade. It flowers from late summer into autumn, with simple, single white blooms that are intriguingly tinged with green. It can easily reach three meters tall but it needn't become unruly; to prune it, you can just chop it back in spring to 10cm (4in) from ground level.

The beautifully fragrant common jasmine (*Jasminum officinale*) is perhaps the archetypal cottage garden climber and one of the most vigorous, but it can work in a small garden and even in a large container provided it is pruned annually after flowering. It flowers from summer into early autumn, so in a small garden it is best given a partner than can stretch the season of interest.

Less vigorous than jasmine but with equally beautiful, understated

Training climbing roses such as The Generous Gardener horizontally gives a display that shows flowers all over the plant, rather than just at the top.

flowers is the rather unflatteringly named potato vine, *Solanum laxum* (or *jasminoides*) 'Album'. Rest assured it has far more elegance than a potato. Its floppy stems need supporting, but when it produces its clusters of simple white star-shaped flowers with lemon yellow centres, the effort proves worthwhile. It is borderline hardy, so best for growing against a warm, sheltered house wall where it may hold onto its leaves all winter.

*Clematis vitalba* flowers elegantly at the same time, with finely split flowers that look as if they have had their petals trimmed with scissors. After flowering it produces the most exquisite seedheads that can look a real picture and add interest to a large wall in winter. This is a scrambling, vigorous climber that can reach 30m (98ft) so best for a very large garden, unless you hack it back each year to keep to around 5m (16ft).

## HERBS

Herbs play a part in the romantic vision of a traditional cottage garden. In addition to their use in the kitchen (and earlier, the apothecary), they are attractive plants in their own right and amiable bedfellows for shrubs and perennials. Mediterranean herbs also grow well in containers and will not complain if you forget to water them.

The earliest cottage gardeners also grew vegetables, as a matter of practicality, and if, like me, your passion for gardening comes from memories of that first plant grown, then you may find a place for the odd vegetable plant in your own modern cottage garden. The first plant I ever grew was a courgette and although it withered and died prematurely, it started a habit of growing these plants that I still continue with. They are not the greatest of subjects for an ornamental garden because they take up so much space, but vegetables such as swiss chard, rhubarb, and globe artichokes add good colour and structure to the garden without making it look agricultural.

**Borage** (*Borago officinalis*) is invaluable. Its clusters of pale blue flowers, blooming in profusion, are tremendous for attracting bees to the garden. Borage grows well in free-draining soil, making it a natural partner for sharp blue eryngiums, both of which will encourage more bees and look good in the garden until winter.

**Chives** (*Allium schoenoprasum*), a beautiful addition, thrive in moist soil, their miniature flowerheads like a shrunken version of taller, large-flowered alliums such as 'Globemaster' but no less beautiful for their diminutive stature. They provide a vivid shot of colour to the garden in early summer without any need to worry about the flower stems blowing over in windy conditions. This makes them good for containers in exposed situations where flower stems of taller alliums in pots can easily fall over. The flowerheads can be kept intact to give the garden winter structure too.

**Feverfew** (*Parthenium* species) is a free-flowering herb with all the charm of bygone days as it shows off daisy-like yellow flowers in summer and autumn. It is a prolific self-seeder if the soil is moist, so some plants may need pulling out in spring.

Lavender is a stalwart plant of many traditional cottage garden plantings.

**Lavender** (*Lavandula* species) is the mainstay of many a cottage garden and often the choice for a low hedge. It thrives on free-draining, stony

soil and full sun and can work beautifully well planted with perennial wallflowers or alchemilla, which thrive in identical conditions. Aside from its flowers, its structural merits include subtle grey-green, late-summer foliage that provides a neat contrast with the dull green of old leaves of echinacea, rudbeckia, and hardy geraniums.

**Rosemary** (*Rosmarinus officinalis*) is a dependable evergreen for providing year-round structure. Careful harvesting of the shoots to keep the plant in a compact shape will give it more impact and prevent the leggy growth that rosemary is prone to as the plant gets a couple of years old. Prune it back by up to a third after flowering to keep it in a tight shape. Its drought tolerance makes rosemary a valuable evergreen for pots (some evergreens such as box and yew are far thirstier and forever drying out in pots, with the brown foliage to prove it), where regular clipping will help keep it from taking over the display. Its spring flowers look decidedly summery and will have lots of impact in a mixed container.

**Santolina or cotton lavender** (*Santolina chamaecyparissus*), another silver-leaved herb, has a lot to offer. Clip it back after flowering and it forms a tight dome that adds structure to containers and borders. Its rich buttery yellow flowers smother the plant when they appear in early summer. Santolina is a sun-loving, drought-tolerant herb that looks good alongside plants with glaucous blue leaves.

**Thyme** is a wonderful ornamental, creating a bushy mound of early summer blossom that bees will feast on. Try planting it on a well-drained border edge and mingling it among roses, because the first flush of most roses coincides with thyme being in full bloom. Although thyme is a Mediterranean herb suited to dry conditions and light soil, it will still grow in heavier soil provided that it drains well. Common thyme (*Thymus vulgaris*) makes an attractive dome-shaped plant with more impact than creeping thyme (*Thymus serpyllum*).

# CARING FOR THE GARDEN IN SUMMER

Although spring may feel like the busiest month for the gardener, summer is the most crucial if a fair proportion of the garden is taken up with new plants and plants growing in containers. In a hot summer, watering alone can take up more time than the frenzy of planting, sowing, and cutting back that sparks gardeners to life in spring. But it is never a chore, as the more you have to water in the garden, the more closely you get to appreciate the quirks and constant development of the plants.

## To-do list for summer

☐ Cut back the old tatty leaves of hardy geraniums to get a flush of lush new growth and in some cases a few more flowers.

☐ Cut back climbers that are outgrowing their space. Don't worry about losing flowers if they are encroaching too much or casting unwanted shade—be ruthless!

☐ Early in the morning or late in the evening, water plants younger than two years old in hot and dry conditions.

☐ Place saucers underneath thirsty pots to avoid wasting water and to keep the plant's roots cool (think twice about doing this if you have a rodent problem—the standing water will attract them during dry spells).

Tie new shoots of climbers to their supports to help them cover boundaries more quickly.

☐ Shorten overly long stems that are spoiling the shape of woody shrubs, cutting them back just above a leaf so they are in proportion with the rest of the plant.

☐ Plant summer-flowering half-hardy annual plants once the risk of frost has passed.

☐ Tie in wayward shoots of climbers that aren't growing towards their supports or their allotted spaces.

Deadhead plants ruthlessly to encourage more flowers to appear and to sharpen up the display of plants in containers. Removing a handful of dull flowers instantly lifts the display.

## WATERING

All plants need a thorough soaking after planting: water until puddles form on the soil surface. After that, there is a real art to watering, and knowing when to water comes with repetition and practice. Most plants grown direct in the soil will depend on the gardener to give them extra water in the first two years after planting. By the third year, they should have developed an extensive enough root system to fend for themselves unless conditions are very hot and dry in summer. Spreading a mulch of compost or composted bark around the base of the plant after the first watering will help the plant hold on to moisture and keep the roots cool, which will reduce the need for watering.

If a plant's leaves are starting to pale in colour and shrivel in summer, then this is a sure sign that it needs water. Other plants such as evergreen shrubs show no external symptoms when they are under stress from drought, so you will need to check the moisture of the compost or soil. For plants in pots, if the compost is pale and dusty, then the plants most likely need watering. Push your finger into the compost and if it is dry all the way down, then watering is needed. Get in the habit of checking plants each evening in summer; then if they need water you can provide it

Water containers in the cool of the evening or early in the morning in summer to help the plants conserve moisture.

straightaway without the risk of it quickly evaporating in the midday sun. For their whole lives you will have to water plants in containers in the same way as plants that are less than two years old in the ground.

## CHELSEA CHOP

Giving plants the Chelsea chop is simple, but pruning in this way can be an agonizing task for gardeners because it involves lopping off a lot of lush new growth that you spent all winter hoping and praying to see one day. And unlike a lot of gardening tasks, it doesn't fall into the be-cruel-to-be-kind category. You don't have to do the Chelsea chop. If you leave the plants alone they do just fine. So why put yourself through the pain?

First, it will make some of your plants more compact and bushy, and less likely to be blown over in strong winds or to look out of proportion in the border. But the real pay-off is that the Chelsea chop will cheat the normal flowering season and you will have fresh blooms for longer. For example, if you have two specimens of *Sedum* 'Autumn Joy' in the garden and you give the Chelsea chop to one and not the other, then you will have one plant bursting into flower at the usual time and another bursting into full bloom maybe four to six weeks later, so you can enjoy fresher flowers for longer.

And why is it called the Chelsea chop? This is because it is traditionally carried out towards the end of May in the UK, which is when the Royal Horticultural Society's Chelsea Flower Show takes place in London. Maybe it should be called the early summer chop to avoid any confusion.

## PRUNING SHRUBS

Lots of gardeners are scared of pruning plants at the wrong time, but it's always worth asking what is the worst that can happen. The notion of there being a wrong time to prune a shrub just stems from the fact that if you prune some shrubs at certain times, then you may not get as many flowers. The chances of killing a plant by pruning it are no higher than killing it by under- or overwatering or by planting it in unsuitable soil. The end product of this concern is normally a hesitancy to prune plants as well as they could be pruned. Just trimming a plant to play it safe is an understandable fallback option if you think you might lose the plant if you get things wrong, but plants treated in this way will often end up looking unnatural, as if they have been forced into a shape even if the shape doesn't have deliberately straight lines.

If a shrub produces its flowers on stems from the previous year, then the best time to prune is immediately after flowering, so that the plant has time to produce new shoots that will mature and flower in the following year. If a shrub flowers on new growth, then prune it at the start of the growing season.

# Autumn

There is something both sad and uplifting about the onset of autumn, but this is the season when the melding of two planting styles really pays off. The strong colours of late-flowering perennials such as asters, heleniums, and coreopsis, coupled with the muted but complex colours of grasses such as *Libertia peregrinans*, *Carex buchananii*, and *Stipa tenuissima* gain a new dimension in the company of persistent repeat-flowering roses, bee-friendly catmint, and airy *Erigeron karvinskianus*.

The sage shades of autumn are blended with the soft pastels still being pumped out by many cottage garden plants. It is not just leaf colours that start to change from the norm either. Subtle changes in the hues of summer flowers you thought so familiar will begin to take hold as days shorten and mornings are thick with dew.

Autumn somehow manages to be the season of both familiarity and unexpected changes. The leaves turn from green to auburn shades as expected—but we have no idea what the exact colours of autumn will be. Unlike the first rose of summer, the first leaf hues of autumn keep us guessing and remind us that even the most regimented and religious of gardeners is ultimately as powerless as King Canute to decide on the colour palette that autumn will present them with.

Maturing foliage glows in the sun to give a full-bodied backdrop for flowers that are new to the garden for the year —such as the pink, dome-shaped flowerheads of *Sedum* 'Autumn Joy'—and those that have been

Molinias and asters intertwine in the border in autumn as the garden becomes a riot of both colour and texture and foliage starts to age.

present for months (erysimums, roses, and calibrachoas). The garden has never been as full, with many plants unrecognizable from their appearance only four months earlier. Looking at the garden in autumn and comparing it to the start of summer is like meeting youthful relatives after a long absence and not believing how much they have grown up and changed.

Growing shrubs and perennials that keep flowering until frost stops them in their tracks will enable the garden to look as colourful as it did in spring. That feeling of freshness and new life will be gone, but autumn brings its own atmosphere to the garden. It is a season of both reflection and celebration; like a birthday party for an ageing loved one. Life is celebrated and time has made the celebrant richer, more colourful, and multilayered.

## LATE-FLOWERING PERENNIALS

Many perennial flowers are associated with the new perennial style of planting, most blooming from midsummer onwards, which is a real bonus for anyone whose traditional cottage garden flowers enter a fallow period by the second month of summer. By autumn the prairie perennials are still going strong, providing a celebratory atmosphere to the garden,

**Above:** Gardens are never fuller than in autumn when herbaceous perennials are at their optimum size and grasses stretch out to their full height.

**Opposite:** As summer turns to autumn, echinaceas and coreopsis add strong tones to the garden as the colour palette becomes more intense.

a kind of joyous thanksgiving service for the exuberance of summer and a feeling of a colourful new era beginning.

In early autumn, the strong suits of the new perennial movement come out all guns blazing. Those that made their presence felt towards the end of summer by beginning to bloom— *Echinacea purpurea* 'Magnus', *Coreopsis grandiflora* 'Early Sunrise', *Salvia nemorosa* 'Caradonna'—are still going strong and look wonderful when knitted together with wispy foliage that shimmers in the autumn winds to make a moving backdrop for brighter colours.

Echinacea has long been a prairie favourite and an explosion in the range of hues that are available makes it possible to grow them in almost

any colour scheme. Perhaps the perfect candidate for the modern cottage garden is the reliable 'Magnus', which shows off the distinctive parasol-shaped echinacea blooms with swept-back petals in a fetching shade of soft pink that will collide with the flowering time of similarly shaded cottage garden perennials such as red valerian (*Centranthus ruber*).

Many perennial plants that flower late in summer and well into autumn produce hot colours: oranges, reds, and buttery yellows. Appealing effortlessly to both the cottage garden and new perennial planting styles, heleniums like damp soil and as a result tend to attract interest from slugs and snails, but once plants start to grow strongly in early summer, they provide a profusion of cheerful flowers that work so well with other plants.

Heleniums add some bright colour to borders in autumn, mingling well with the more muted shades of ageing grasses.

Try growing them around rudbeckias, geums, cosmos, and red hot pokers (*Kniphofia*). *Helenium autumnale* 'Helena Red Shades' has flowers in deepest red, while 'Sahin's Early Flowerer' is orange fading to buttery yellow. Forming fairly loose clumps and making slightly dome-shaped plants, heleniums are perfect partners for growing among roses, allowing for countless different colour combinations.

**Above right:** Asters give the garden a vibrant injection of colour and contrast beautifully with the ever-changing tones of deciduous hedgerows.

**Below:** Rudbeckias and chrysanthemums present a perfect mix of new perennial and cottage garden style when grown together in a container or in the ground in the garden.

Towards the end of the season it is the turn of asters such as soft pink *Aster* 'Kylie' to give the garden a lift, while the pink and purple varieties make a spectacular show when paired with sedums or the late flowers of a rich pink rose such as Gertrude Jekyll for some complimentary colour. 'Kylie' (or *Symphyotrichum novae-angliae* 'Kylie') is a New England aster, which is the type that stays free from mildew. With their light, almost luminous show of colour, these asters also make a fine contrast if planted against a background of deciduous hedges and trees, the vibrant and the burnished making a fine pairing. Snip back the tip of each shoot by up to half in early summer for a shorter, bushier plant.

And for a loud end-of-season clash, also try growing asters among perennial rudbeckias. Perennial rudbeckias also blend well with hardy perennial chrysanthemums, particularly the double-flowered forms,

with a beautiful contrast between the simplicity of the rudbeckia and the fussiness of the chrysanthemum.

For more autumn colour contrasts, the curious sub-shrub *Ceratostigma plumbaginoides* adds some wonderfully rich colour to the season. With flowers somewhere between a vinca and a hardy geranium but smaller, this is a fine groundcover plant that looks pretty but unremarkable in summer until transforming in autumn. Its leaves take on beautiful shades of red and purple and it continues to flower at the same time. Its growth is neat and compact and will be enhanced by golden grasses that can cascade above it (try *Hakonechloa macra* 'Alboaurea' or *Carex oshimensis* 'Evergold') for a sharp contrast with the autumn colour. Or for something that blends, try the red autumn strands of red tussock grass (*Chionochloa rubra*).

## GRASSES

Grasses are the perfect plants for knitting together plants in the garden, and it could be argued that autumn is their peak season. With the sun lower and weaker than in summer and grasses standing tall and flowering, there is ample opportunity for silhouettes to be sharpened by shafts of sunlight when many deciduous forms start to produce shades of orange and red as their leaves age.

Allied with the pastels of asters, roses, and erysimums, autumn can be as colourful as summer in the garden, with the colours more nuanced and a richness and depth that is missed in summer. The good thing about most grasses is that you don't need a lot of space in the garden to fit them in, and the closer they grow to other plants, the more visual impact they have as their colours complement or stand out against others.

Grasses can act like the lines in a dot-to-dot, joining up the gaps between flowering plants to complete an intricate and detailed picture that would have otherwise been a chaotic jumble. And in autumn many deciduous grasses give their own spectacular light show as low sun accentuates the rich diversity of colours found in both their leaves and flowers as they become more flamboyant with age (this is sometimes true of gardeners too). If you have the chance to plant grasses in an open, west-facing position, grab it with both arms—or should that be both spades? As the low sun hits the foliage it will cast them in an ethereal morning or evening glow.

The foliage of grasses—such as *Libertia perigrinans*, which shows shades of orange, red, and green together, and *Panicum virgatum* 'Rehbraun', which becomes streaked with red—changes dramatically as the summer turns to autumn, and the changing hues as the sun

**Above:** Autumn is the time when grasses and perennials collide to show sharp contrasts in the border.

**Above right:** Grasses start to glow in the garden in autumn and provide a backdrop to show off the darkening seedheads of flowering perennials.

hits them create new colour combinations that change not just by the day but by the minute.

Tall grasses will help provide a feathery backdrop for colourful lower-growing flowering perennials, and shorter grasses planted around the front of a border can help hide the nether regions of plants that become scruffy towards the end of summer. The bases of roses can become bare as leaves fall and the leaves of Shasta daisies (*Leucanthemum*) start to turn sickly late in the season, especially if the soil is light. Try the grass *Stipa tenuissima* at the front of the border to act as a screen for old foliage. When in flower, the plant produces a thick, sleek mane of growth that gives a full and frothy appearance if you grow a few of these plants close together.

Many grasses create a fine show of flowers in autumn and they make a tremendous backdrop for a border, their blooms like an explosion of sparks from a firework. Perhaps the most spectacular is *Stipa gigantea* with its sprays of straw-coloured flowers that reach up to two and half meters tall. If this will look out of place in your garden because of its height, try *Miscanthus sinensis* Red Cloud which bears loose heads of pink-purple-tinged, tassel-like flowers among, fine, wispy foliage and grows to a more modest meter tall. For something slightly taller, try *Miscanthus sinensis* 'Morning Light', which grows to a meter and a half and has the most unobtrusive, beautifully slender leaves.

## PERENNIALS

Many classic perennials also bring spectacular hues to the garden in autumn. In summer *Bergenia* 'Bressingham Ruby' won't stand out from the crowd, but in autumn its broad leaves (when I was a child they were always called elephant's ears in our garden) start to turn a beautiful maroon and it will become a border highlight. On closer inspection of the leaves you will notice a softly serrated edge to them and the undersides will glow bright red in the sun. A mainstay of a traditional cottage garden, bergenias that have been allowed to spread are big on impact. A ground-cover plant, it will look tremendous growing at the base of grasses such as *Sesleria caerulea* or *Carex oshimensis* 'Evergold'.

Another perennial with gorgeous red autumn colouring is *Epimedium ×perralchicum* 'Fröhnleiten' (you'll get the hang of the name eventually). Its shield-shaped leaves display prominent lime-green veins as the leaves turn to wine red, providing both a fresh and burnished look to the garden in an area of dry shade.

And of course shrubs that produce spectacular autumn foliage will add extra interest to the garden in winter. Choose carefully though because shrubs can take up significant space, and if autumn is their only season of interest it may not justify the amount of ground they demand.

For autumn berries rather than leaves, the graceful shrub *Leycesteria formosa* (sometimes called pheasant berry or Himalayan honeysuckle) bears clusters of hanging purple berries with dark red caps in autumn, held elegantly among gently hanging stems. It forms a tall, bushy shrub

**Above right:** *Epimedium ×perralchicum* 'Fröhnleiten' adds the same mix of vibrant and subdued colours to the garden in both spring and autumn.

**Right:** The autumn shades on the leaves of *Nandina domestica* 'Firepower' add a complexity to the edge of a border, where this useful plant grows to around 45cm (1ft 6in) tall.

but can be cut back to just above ground level in spring to control its size. It is hardy down to -15°C (5°F).

*Nandina domestica* 'Firepower' is a plant with colourful autumn foliage that won't take up too much room, makes a big impact in containers, and looks good in more than one season. In autumn it glows in shades of bright red, yellow-green, and bleached orange. In spring the new growth is flushed with an orangey red before taking on a pink hue then fading to lime-green.

For perhaps the brightest autumn colouring possible, the leaves of *Euonymus europaeus* 'Red Cascade' produce the most intense mix of strawberry red and purple before they fall. This euonymus also bears orangey pink fruits at the end of summer, which last through winter to add some splashes of late colour. Plant a light-pink-flowered aster such as *A. ×frikartii* 'Wunder von Stäfa' with it to create an eye-catching contrast.

# CARING FOR THE GARDEN IN AUTUMN

This season is something of a loveable rogue. Dazzling colours come and go quickly, while rich, deep shades of foliage and flower are displayed amid mist, fog, and the faded glory of summer's worn-out plants. The amount of tidying to be done in the garden while so many plants are in transition is all a case of personal preference (the truth is that some of us are tidier gardeners than others), but the following tasks will all make a big difference to your garden, some immediately, some in years to come.

## To-do list for autumn

☐ Continue deadheading annuals and perennials but leave intact the flower-heads that will look pretty in frosty weather and provide structure in winter.

☐ Pull out tatty-looking and diseased annual plants that are past their best.

Check late-flowering perennials in flower for any dead foliage and remove it before planting so that water can get down to the roots of the plants easily when they are watered.

Plant autumn-flowering plants and evergreens in containers to give patio areas an instant lift and colour for the rest of the season.

☐ Clean the outside of patio containers using a stiff brush and warm, soapy water to keep patio areas looking fresh and vibrant.

☐ Prune back the flowered shoots on late-summer-flowering shrubs that have finished flowering.

☐ On a cool evening in damp conditions, move perennial plants that are growing in the wrong place.

☐ Plant new perennials when the soil is damp and the weather is cool.

☐ Plant spring-flowering bulbs in among evergreen grasses and shrubs in borders, mixing in grit to the bottom of the planting holes in heavy soil.

Keep the roots intact with as much soil attached as possible when moving plants.

## PREPARING THE SOIL

It is difficult to quickly make a light soil heavier—it will take years of applications of well-rotted horse manure or homemade compost. It is also very difficult to make a highly acidic soil alkaline or vice versa. But heavy soils can be lightened instantly by the addition of horticultural grit or sand. Mix the grit or sand in well rather than placing it at the base of planting holes; otherwise the material can act as a sump.

## MOVING PLANTS

This is a gardening task nowhere near as fraught with danger as many gardeners seem to think. Yes, you might want to think twice about moving a reasonably old tree or a plant that was expensive or has a high sentimental value, but otherwise, moving plants is an essential trick to have up your sleeve to greatly enhance the look of your garden.

The end of autumn is a good time to move perennials because there is a dampness in the air and temperatures have cooled sufficiently to not stress moved plants, but it is warm enough for the plant to get settled before winter. Winter is the perfect time to move woody plants such as roses and shrubs, but autumn is better for perennials when they still have a lot of growth on show. This means that you can move them when you can see why the plant doesn't work in its current position. You may have forgotten in spring, when perennials are only just emerging and not showing signs of how much space they will take up later in the year. It's amazing how the human mind forgets these things in a different season of the year.

The trick with moving any plant is to prepare the planting hole in the position that you want to move the plant to, before you dig the plant up. This way it can simply be dropped straight into the new planting hole with the minimum of disturbance, and the roots aren't out of the soil or exposed for very long. Water immediately after planting and do it on a cool evening so that there is no risk of the plant being exposed to warm temperatures straight after moving.

When digging up and moving a plant, it's best not to dig too close to the crown of the plant, and if the soil is reasonably heavy, use a fork rather than a spade to avoid severing many roots. Push the fork as deep down as you can all around the plant to try and keep as much soil intact around the rootball as possible and to avoid breaking roots as well.

# Winter

There's no hiding from the difficulty of winter in the garden. The time for observing is shortened by cold air, saturated soil, and lingering darkness. The garden, a place that transfixed us every day only weeks ago, can slip down the list of priorities and become an afterthought, a place to return to again when the next season arrives and the weather warms up.

It doesn't have to be this way though. To every gardener's frustration, nothing can be done about the weather but dormancy is part of the rhythm of nature and it does us good to have time to reflect on the garden, the plants that have worked and the planting combinations that have brought a new lease of life to plants that we thought we knew well.

Winter in the garden is not just a time for reflection and whimsy though, because there is still much to be enjoyed, to lift the spirits amid the damp and cold. Imagine drawing the curtains in the morning in winter, looking out at the garden, and being as excited to go out there as you were in high summer. Maybe that isn't possible, but the garden can still be an attractive place to look at in winter.

Winter is when the garden can play a three-card trick, showing off the vivid hues of evergreens and coloured stems, the monochrome beauty of summer's faded glory, and the freshness of simple scented flowers. If summer is the party season in the garden, then winter is the best-kept secret, only truly discovered by the creative and inquisitive gardener.

The form of fading perennials is transformed by frost, while rose hips and honeysuckle berries provide shots of colour and viewing material for

Piet Oudolf's Millennium Garden at Pensthorpe Natural Park in Norfolk, UK, is left completely intact until the end of winter.

birdwatchers. Structural evergreens help break up thickets of old growth with colours that stand out from a distance, and the frosted reminders of summer's star plants provide us with next year's hope.

This is the season when you will be glad that you didn't decide to snip off the flowers of perennials and grasses for the sake of tidiness. These old flowers that were looking fatigued in autumn are now given a new lease of life to once again become highlights in the border. The once purple-pink domed flowerheads of *Sedum* 'Matrona' take on shades of maroon and dark brown as they stand unmoved from the glory of late summer, iden-tical in size and stature, a perfectly preserved relic of a lost season. Pair them with a taller, shimmering grass such as *Sporobolus heterolepis* to

**Above:** The wavy shafts of *Sporobolus heterolepis* contrast nicely with the solid structure of the flower stems of *Sedum* 'Matrona' below and *Echinacea purpurea* 'Rubinglow' above.

**Above right:** *Calamagrostis brachytricha* still shows its graceful shape in the garden right through to the end of winter.

show off its silhouette and create a colour contrast that is more subtle than summer's but perhaps even more effective because of the interest it brings in the depths of winter when growth has long halted.

It may be too cold to do much gardening, but there will be much to admire on a walk through a modern cottage garden. Keeping planting areas intact in winter allows all the combinations of form and foliage to be enjoyed. When frost captures the garden in winter, it will be seen almost in black and white but a rich diversity of form makes a fine and distinguished substitute for colour.

Some grasses are incredibly durable and will stand tall and add structure and form to a border all through winter, regardless of storms and

Dark stems of perennials kept intact over winter such as *Astilbe chinensis* var. *taquetii* 'Purpurlanze' stand out well behind straw-coloured grasses.

cold weather. *Calamagrostis brachytricha* keeps its shape beautifully, with its slender flowerheads gracefully arching over a border at around 1.2m (4ft). And even parts of the border that are damp in winter can show some architectural reminders of summer and autumn. The stout summer flower stems of astilbes such as *Astilbe chinensis* var. *taquetii* 'Purpurlanze' take on a reddish brown hue and stand out beautifully as silhouettes behind an ageing mass of deciduous grasses.

Rose hips add a shot of late colour to the muted shades around the garden. The slender strawberry-red hips of *Rosa glauca* will lift the mono-chrome scene of ageing seedheads of *Eutrochium* (or *Eupatorium*) *maculatum* or varieties of *Rudbeckia fulgida*, and in the winter they serve as a staging post for birds to come and feed on, along with the neighbouring seedheads.

Plants with colourful winter stems can also add a vibrancy to the ghostly remnants of deciduous grasses and late-flowering perennials. The beauty of these plants, such as orangey yellow *Cornus sanguinea* 'Midwinter Fire' or deep red-stemmed *Cornus alba*, is that their colour becomes more evident as winter deepens, leaves fall, and the landscape becomes barer. Plant bright evergreen grasses such as *Carex oshimensis* 'Evergold' beneath them for even more colour in winter.

## EVERGREEN SHRUBS

Let's be honest: evergreen shrubs don't exactly set the pulses racing. They are rarely the plants that provoke a "wow" reaction on first sight and are seldom the result of an impulse buy at the nursery. Yet we probably don't get excited about buying eggs even though the result-ing pancakes, omelet, or home-baked cakes wouldn't be the same without them. So it is with evergreen shrubs; the modern cottage garden needs them. They are an integral part of the recipe for success, with a role to play in keeping the garden well-structured. Tall-growing ever-greens such as *Viburnum tinus* are also useful for framing areas of flowering plants, and it will look pretty when caught by a frost in winter, when the flowers are still in their pink buds.

*Viburnum tinus* provides welcome structure to the garden all through the year and looks especially good in winter when in bud and flower.

Inevitably evergreen plants are going to be noticed more than most plants at this time of year, and keeping them well-shaped will make a big difference to the overall look of the garden. Even though the modern cottage garden is hardly formal in style, dome-shaped evergreens such as *Pittosporum tenuifolium* 'Tom Thumb' that don't quite have a crisp edge will look like they should have one.

Using evergreens that form different shapes will keep the garden looking diverse and interesting through winter. The idea of keeping repetition to a minimum can be applied to evergreens too because it is easy to overdo and rely too much on them for winter colour. If you grow more than one of the same evergreen, try pruning them to different heights so they look like completely different garden features.

Shrubs will also provide a fine supporting role for other colourful winter plants. *Euonymus fortunei* 'Emerald 'n' Gold' and 'Silver Queen' are so often block-planted in municipal areas that they are deemed not worthy of a place in many gardens, but used sparingly around the base of a brightly coloured dogwood (*Cornus* species) or a deciduous grass that is glowing in the evening sun, they add their own vibrancy to the garden in winter after going almost unnoticed in summer. They are both compact shrubs that can be pruned at any time if they outgrow their space.

*Euonymus fortunei* 'Silver Queen' will grow in almost any soil, and its fresh variegated foliage will lighten up a border without ever taking the limelight.

Cotton lavender grows well in dry, stony soil and provides summer colour, its ageing seedheads then offering extra interest in autumn and winter.

Evergreen shrubs become more obvious in winter and can look especially fine if trimmed to a sharp edge ready to be tinged with frost, but they can also be incorporated into the colour scheme of the garden in summer. The buttery yellow pompon flowers of cotton lavender (*Santolina chamaecyparissus*) will work wonderfully well with different shades of orange and yellow achilleas, and the plant also bears attractive seedheads for autumn and winter structure. Try bright yellow *Achillea* 'Moonshine' for a near perfect match in summer, or burnt orange 'Terracotta' for a pleasing complementary tone.

Other evergreens will bring their own seasonal highlights to the border. The creamy white flowers of *Phillyrea angustifolia*, which form in clusters all the way along the stems starting at the base of the leaves, offer a delicious summer scent. For a later show of scented white blossom from an evergreen shrub, grow *Osmanthus fragrans* (fragrant olive) if you have a position in the border that is sheltered from cold winds or if you have a gap by a warm wall. It is hardy down to around -15°C (5°F).

For bright colour as well as form in winter, some evergreen grasses will really stand out, especially if they have broad leaves. Colourful *Luzula sylvatica* 'Aurea' adds a golden glow and will gently cascade over the edge of a border or a container in winter.

Shrubs that flower in winter are often highly fragrant, but choose them with care and use them sparingly if you have a small garden because they can become big plants and some don't offer a lot to the garden for the rest of the year. Also make sure to plant them where you can enjoy the scent, such as by the edge of a path or in a container near an entrance to the house or garage. Among the finest and a superb partner for rusty coloured evergreen grasses such as *Carex testacea* are witchhazels such as the fiery orange and red *Hamamelis ×intermedia* 'Jelena'. The spidery flowers release a spicy scent and produce a depth of colour that will keep photography enthusiasts busy.

Perhaps its main rival in the winter scent department is *Daphne bholua* 'Jacqueline Postill' which will stop many a passer-by in their tracks as they try and work out what is smelling so divine on a drab winter's day. When the plant is in full bloom, showing off pale pink flowers clustered among deep pink buds, you can feel as though it is showing you a photo of a garden plant in summer. It is semi-evergreen but planting a bright-leaved luzula or a variegated ivy beneath it will create a fuller scene.

An easy winter-flowering shrub to find room for in the garden is *Abeliophyllum distichum*, which grows to a fairly modest meter and a half tall, so it can be woven into a gap in the border. It is sometimes labeled as white forsythia because its flowers are a similar shape to those of forsythia. Its simple, single white blooms clothe the upright stems as if they were spring blossom, and it will provide a cool, fresh contrast with the greys and browns of fading perennial foliage around it.

## CARING FOR THE GARDEN IN WINTER

The beauty of the modern cottage garden in winter is that there is still much to enjoy looking at, and as you gaze on the frosted, monochrome remains of summer and autumn's most colourful plants, it is a season of reflection rather than busyness. But there are still some tasks that are best done in winter when weather allows and the season comes to a welcome close, with the promise of spring around the corner.

## To-do list for winter

☐ Snip off the old flowerheads from summer-flowering perennials when the flower stalks start to fall and look tatty.

☐ Prune roses before they start to produce new shoots so that they will flower nice and early in summer. Later pruning will mean later flowers.

☐ Once their form has been spoiled by strong winds or heavy rains, cut back deciduous grasses to 5cm (2in) above ground level.

☐ Move evergreen plants in pots to prominent positions by doorways and windows so they can be appreciated at close quarters.

☐ Use a hand fork to comb out the dead material from evergreen grasses before spring arrives and the plant makes new shoots.

Place pots onto pot feet to allow water to drain through them well.

## CUTTING THE GARDEN BACK

Hands up who likes to do a good old garden blitz? You know what I mean. Every plant within a lopper's radius gets chopped, weeds are attacked with gusto, soil is broken up and raked to a fine tilth, and even the lawn gets edged if there's time before dark. If time is at a premium then this is often how practical gardening happens, and the good news is that the modern cottage garden is suited to being given a good blitz of cutting plants back at the end of winter.

A big change that the new perennial planting style has bought to gardening is the timing of cutting back the old growth on perennial plants. Before the style arrived, most gardeners would tidy up their garden and cut everything back once the summer flowers had gone. The new approach of leaving everything intact so that planting areas still have form and structure in winter can be hard to stick to if you like to always be doing things in the garden and if you find it hard not to get carried away cutting things back (and let's be honest, isn't that every gardener?), but the result of timely restraint is a garden that looks beautiful for longer.

The easiest way to look after a prairie-style planting scheme is to leave everything in place until the prominent parts of the garden that looked spectacular when decorated by frost have shrivelled or turned to mush (it happens to us all eventually).

Then once the winter show is over and the soil starts to warm up in spring—the emergence of annual weed seedlings is a good indicator of this—all the old leaves and stems are cut back to just above ground level and removed to make way for new growth and to set up prairie-style plantings for the new season.

There are many benefits to this timing in the modern cottage garden. Leaving old material intact over winter will protect the crowns of plants, which is valuable for plants that may get killed off by a very cold winter, and will also protect young shoots that emerge early as a result of an unusual mild spell. Keeping everything in place sets the stage for the spectacular winter show when the frost arrives and allows you to appreciate the form and structure of plants in their dormancy.

Leave the growth of deciduous grasses intact until the end of winter, then cut it back as close to ground level as possible using shears.

Prune back the old seedheads on perennials at the end of winter after they have had the chance to be highlighted by frost.

If the thought of cutting back the plant to nothing seems daunting, wait until you see the first new shoots of spring—telling you that the plant is still alive—and then cut back the plant. It will soon produce new shoots. Evergreen grasses just need a tidy-up in spring by combing or raking out old, tatty-looking leaves. If the plant is full of old leaves, then you can do a renovation prune, chopping all the old growth down to just above ground level in spring, and it will respond by producing new shoots.

## PRUNING ROSES

The ideal time to prune a rose is before it has started to produce new shoots. Don't be put off by the thought of cutting back a plant that isn't showing any signs of new growth. Pruning a rose before the first leaf buds of the year have broken will result in the plants flowering as early as possible in late spring or early summer. If pruning is delayed until a rose has produced shoots that have almost made it to fully formed leaves, then the plant will have to go back to square one and start all over again. It's a bit like walking to your car, getting ready to pull away, and realizing that you've left your glasses indoors. You have to repeat your steps and cover the same ground again.

Some gardeners are hesitant to choose a rose for their garden because of the myth that pruning roses is complicated. It really isn't. They are some of the easiest plants to prune.

Just chop back each stem as far as you want to. If you want a small plant then cut it back to 10cm (4in) from ground level in early spring. If you want a taller, more substantial plant that will grow in the middle or near the back of a border, then cut it back by between a third and two-thirds. Also cut back to healthy green growth any stems that are dead or going brown.

Old rose bushes that have developed thick stems will thank you if you cut out around a quarter of the old stems completely at the base. This will improve the plant's shape, allow air to flow, and produce a tidier plant that doesn't look like an impenetrable thicket.

Climbers and ramblers are easy to prune too. When rambling roses have finished flowering (usually after one big flush of blossom in summer), just chop back any stems that have outgrown their space. Climbers that have more than one flush of flowers are best pruned back at the same time as bush roses, but only prune if you have to: it's far better to fan out the stems horizontally and tie them to their supports to make a broad, impressive plant. If any stems are growing in the wrong direction and simply refuse to be trained in the way that you want them to go (climbing roses can be like small children sometimes), then simply cut them off at ground level.

Hardy fuchsias can be cut back in much the same way as roses. You can be ruthless and chop them back to just above ground level if you want a neat, compact plant that grows to the same height every year. Or just don't cut it back as hard if you want something a bit taller. Bear in mind that as with roses, the stems start to get thicker as they age, so light pruning will eventually result in a plant with a lot of stems that are thick and woody at the base and that may not be as productive.

If your rose bush has started to form new shoots at the end of winter, then it is time to prune out any old, unwanted growth.

## CARING FOR THE GARDEN FOR THE LONGER TERM

If hindsight is truly a wonderful thing, then what word can possibly be used to describe foresight, where a future problem or need is anticipated rather than discovered after the event?

It isn't always easy to predict what will happen in a garden over the longer term. By far the most pressing concern for most gardens over long periods is how much the plants will grow or spread, and whether at some point they will outgrow their space and spoil the look of the garden and the balance of the planting.

Some plants seem to inexplicably grow better than others and some outgrow even the size they were expected to reach. For me, the key to managing a garden as it matures is not to have any fireproof plants that are immune from criticism or from removal.

If a plant just isn't pulling its weight in the garden after a couple of years, then don't be afraid to get rid of it, or move it to another part of the garden to see if it fares any better. It is amazing how many gardeners will allow prominent positions in their gardens to be home to straggly specimens that look like they are trying to survive from a dose of weedkiller. Even if a plant has sentimental value, consider whether it is making your garden look better or worse. And if it has to be kept, is there a quiet corner out of full view where it can be moved to?

Also don't be afraid to drastically reduce the size of perennial plants that are spreading well in the garden, before they take on weed-like status. There is no need to feel bad about digging up and removing unwanted plants, as if you have committed some sort of crime. If you divide a large clump of a plant into ten smaller clumps, there is nothing that says you have to find a home for all ten. Even if you don't have a new home for it or a friend who will take it, it can always be composted to help feed the garden and replenish the soil in the future. A garden where every last straggler is given refuge rarely makes for an eye-catching spectacle.

# 50
# Essential
# Plants

## A to Z

Left to right: *Saxifraga* 'Peter Pan', *Panicum virgatum*,
*Helenium autumnale* 'Helena Red Shades', *Rosa* 'The Pilgrim',
*Spiraea japonica* 'Goldflame', *Agastache* 'Blue Fortune'

The modern cottage garden is a diverse place where plants from across the globe join together to make your yard beautiful. When the style is at its best, there are plants of impact and interest demanding attention throughout the year, some filling a tiny space in a pot, others forming a prominent centrepiece.

I've chosen these fifty plants because I have grown them or have observed them growing in gardens that reflect and celebrate the essence of the modern cottage garden: a long season of interest, a diversity of form and structure, an emphasis on colours that complement each other, and most importantly, a garden space that is entertaining, exciting, and rewarding.

Not all will be to your taste but that is the beauty of the modern cottage garden. It is not dependent on a particular, narrow group of plants. If you love mixing and matching different plants together and you want to create a garden that looks good for long periods, then dive in and experiment with some of these beautiful plants.

## A NOTE ON PLANT CATEGORIES

**Semi-evergreen** refers to a plant that can hold onto its leaves in mild winters or in sheltered spaces, but it may still naturally shed its leaves over winter.

**Herbaceous perennial** refers to a plant that naturally dies down in winter but starts to grow again from ground level in the following spring.

**Borderline hardy perennial** refers to a plant that can normally survive the winter in USDA hardiness zone 6 but may be killed in a very cold or wet winter. Minimum winter temperatures in zone 6 can reach approximately -23°C to -18°C (-10°F to 0°F).

**Borderline hardy shrub** refers to a woody plant that normally survives the winter in zone 6 but may be killed in a very cold or wet winter.

**Hardy annual** and **hardy annual climber** refer to plants that germinate, flower, and die in the same growing season but can be planted or sown in autumn or early spring without being affected by cold weather.

**Half-hardy annual** refers to a plant that germinates, flowers, and dies in the same growing season and should be planted out in the garden once the risk of frost has passed in early summer in zone 6.

**Hardy deciduous shrub** refers to a woody plant that will naturally shed its leaves in winter but will live year after year in zone 6.

## *Agastache* 'Blue Fortune'

Also known as Mexican giant hyssop, agastache is an aromatic-leaved perennial that starts flowering in summer and keeps going until well into autumn. 'Blue Fortune' can be a short-lived plant but well and truly pulls its weight in a sunny, well-drained place. Scores of strong blue bottlebrush flowers are highly attractive to bees; their flower stalks then add vertical interest to the border in winter.

**Plant type** Borderline hardy perennial

**Soil type** Any well-drained soil

**Aspect** Full sun

**Height and spread** 1m × 50cm
(3ft 4in × 1ft 8in)

**Season of interest** Summer and
autumn

## *Alcea rosea* Halo Series

Often seen growing among foxgloves and roses, hollyhocks (*Alcea rosea*) have so much more to offer, and Halo Series flowers have eye-catching centres that contrast in colour with the rest of the blossom. Its stems can be fitted into the smallest of border gaps where they add height and nostalgic charm among heleniums and rudbeckias. Leave the old flowers to seed around and hollyhocks naturally pop up in your border and add a loose cottage garden feel to liven up blocks of prairie perennials. It's a biennial so buy large plants in the first year (or one with flower spikes) so you don't have to wait until the following year for flowers. Multiple colours are sold together as Halo Mix.

**Plant type** Biennial

**Soil type** Damp but well-drained soil

**Aspect** Sun or semi-shade

**Height and spread** 1.4m × 25cm
(4ft 7in × 10in)

**Season of interest** Summer and
early autumn

## Alchemilla epipsila

Lady's mantle (*Alchemilla epipsila*) becomes a border star in early summer when it shows off clouds of yellow-green blossom. The flowers look frothy, frilly, and loose from a distance, but get up close and you will notice the intricate beauty of hundreds of tiny star-shaped blooms. This compact perennial is a classic to pair with roses in early summer because the first flush of roses can coincide well with its flowering time, but it also blends beautifully with fresh shoots of deciduous grasses. Trim off the old flowers if you don't want it to seed around.

**Plant type** Herbaceous perennial

**Soil type** Any well-drained soil

**Aspect** Sun or semi-shade

**Height and spread** 30cm × 30cm
(1ft × 1ft)

**Season of interest** Spring and
summer

## Allium sphaerocephalon

The gorgeous burgundy-red flowerheads of *Allium sphaerocephalon* add some dramatic colour to the garden in high summer, much later and richer in hue than most alliums. The pompon flowers are durable and perfect for leaving intact to contrast with the wispy nature of flowing deciduous grasses in winter and stand proud to be perfectly framed by a hard frost. This is also a real winner planted alongside light pink flowers in a border.

**Plant type** Perennial bulb

**Soil type** Any well-drained soil

**Aspect** Full sun

**Height and spread** 90cm × 50cm
(3ft × 1ft 8in)

**Season of interest** Summer

## *Anemone blanda* 'Blue Shades'

One of the more tasteful early spring flowers, *Anemone blanda* 'Blue Shades' shows off a purplish blue that softens as the flowers age, creating a display that tricks you into thinking that it must be summer. The blooms, although looking delicate, are tough enough to withstand strong winds and rain in spring and retain their elegance; in a cool, shady place 'Blue Shades' can spread well to give the garden a carpet of early colour. It is also perfect for giving the finishing touch to a modern cottage garden container.

**Plant type** Herbaceous perennial

**Soil type** Any damp soil

**Aspect** Shade

**Height and spread** 10cm × 10cm
(4in × 4in)

**Season of interest** Spring

## *Aster ×frikartii* 'Mönch'

Varieties of *Aster ×frikartii* are dependable, healthy perennials for adding both lightness and eye-catching colour to the garden, and especially to add a spark of freshness among the changing hues of ageing autumn foliage. The lavender-blue flowers of 'Mönch' are big for an aster, coming into bloom at the end of summer and continuing well into autumn. The flowers form a large dome, provided the plants are given support early in the growing season.

**Plant type** Hardy perennial

**Soil type** Any well-drained soil

**Aspect** Full sun

**Height and spread** 1m × 50cm
(3ft 4in × 1ft 8in)

## *Brachyglottis* 'Walberton's Silver Dormouse'

'Walberton's Silver Dormouse' is a more compact *Brachyglottis* variety than the popular 'Sunshine', allowing for this soft and silvery shrub to be grown in a container with other plants. Its understated leaves—which have a furry texture—were made for mingling with icy blue eryngium stems and leaves but also prove useful for standing out against darker foliage. If the clouds of bright yellow daisy flowers are too loud for you, just trim them off and grow it for the special, silky foliage alone. It is hardy down to -5°C (23°F).

**Plant type** Borderline hardy shrub

**Soil type** Any well-drained soil

**Aspect** Sun or semi-shade

**Height and spread** 90cm × 1.2m
   (3ft × 4ft)

**Season of interest** All year

## *Brunnera macrophylla* 'Jack Frost'

There is perhaps no daintier plant to grow for spring interest in the garden than *Brunnera macrophylla*. 'Jack Frost' adds pretty spires of powder-blue blossom to light up a damp and shady corner. Its ghostly, silver-patterned leaves provide a nice finishing touch and also serve as a useful weed-suppressor in summer when they are at their largest. A traditional spring perennial to grow with spring-flowering bulbs, it also blends wonderfully with wispy grasses such as *Stipa tenuissima*. Just remember to protect the new shoots from slugs in spring—they must taste nice to them, although deer tend to abstain from the textured leaves.

**Plant type** Herbaceous perennial

**Soil type** Any damp soil

**Aspect** Shade or semi-shade

**Height and spread** 40cm × 60cm
   (1ft 4in × 2ft)

**Season of interest** Spring and summer

## Calamagrostis brachytricha

*Calamagrostis brachytricha*, a graceful grass, adds movement and structure to the garden all year round and forms a robust clump that stands up well until the end of winter, even in exposed situations. Its light and wavy plumes of flowers appear for the first time in late summer and age beautifully, as does the glossy green foliage, which turns yellow in fall before taking on golden hues that glow in the low winter sun.

**Plant type** Deciduous grass

**Soil type** Any soil

**Aspect** Sun or shade

**Height and spread** 1.5m × 1m
(5ft × 3ft 4in)

**Season of interest** All year

## Calendula 'Princess Orange Black'

Exuding both the charm of old-fashioned hardy annuals and the warmth of the boldest prairie perennials, 'Princess Orange Black' is a real high-value plant to grow from seed. Sown direct in the soil in spring, it makes a sprawling, branching plant that will prop itself up on surrounding plants in a border. This variety will produce flower after flower to add hot colour and whimsical charm to a border and is tremendous for filling out a garden in its first year. Keep snipping off the old flowers and it will bloom until the first frosts of winter.

**Plant type** Hardy annual

**Soil type** Any moisture-retentive soil

**Aspect** Sun or semi-shade

**Height and spread** 60cm × 40cm
(2ft × 1ft 4in)

**Season of interest** Summer and autumn

## *Calibrachoa* Cabaret Red Improved

This mini petunia is one of the neatest, most perfectly formed trailing plants to ever grace a container and is more understated and refined than the loud and oversized hybrids that are used in many summer pots. The warm colour of *Calibrachoa* Cabaret Red Improved is also perfect to pair with prairie perennials such as heleniums and rudbeckias. Tolerant of heat and drought, this plant will forgive you for occasionally forgetting to water a container. And like a well-behaved child who even volunteers to wash the plates after lunch, calibrachoas are also self-cleaning, naturally shedding their old flowers so you don't have to deadhead.

**Plant type** Tender perennial

**Soil type** Any well-drained soil

**Aspect** Sun or semi-shade

**Height and spread** 20cm × 30cm (8in × 1ft)

**Season of interest** Summer and autumn

## *Carex oshimensis* Everest

Here is an essential grass for keeping the garden vibrant and colourful in winter. Happy to grow among other plants in pots, *Carex oshimensis* Everest (also called Evercolor Everest) gives the edge of a container a fresh flourish and beautifully softens hard edges of paths and borders as well. If you grow it in light soil and leave the flowers intact, it will easily spread, which is no bad thing, as long as you pull up any unwanted extra plants. An effective plant in summer, it will never steal the show from flowering plants nearby. If you don't have room for Everest, the variety 'Eversheen' looks similar but grows to just 30cm (1ft).

**Plant type** Evergreen grass

**Soil type** Any soil

**Aspect** Sun or shade

**Height and spread** 45cm × 45cm (1ft 6in × 1ft 6in)

**Season of interest** All year

### *Centaurea montana* 'Amethyst in Snow'

The wonderful two-toned flowers of 'Amethyst in Snow' will add a lightness to your garden year after year. *Centaurea montana* is a perennial form of corn-flower, and when the plant is promptly deadheaded it has a long flowering season from spring into summer. It needs to grow in a cool, moist spot in the garden where it will form a compact clump and team up well with brunnera and pulmonaria in spring and then mingle with grasses such as *Carex oshimensis* 'Evergold' through summer.

**Plant type** Herbaceous perennial

**Soil type** Damp but not waterlogged soil

**Aspect** Sun or semi-shade

**Height and spread** 50cm × 50cm (1ft 8in × 1ft 8in)

**Season of interest** Spring and summer

### *Cerinthe major* 'Purpurascens'

It has a reputation for self-seeding, but *Cerinthe major* 'Purpurascens' has a strange beauty that only increases as it multiplies. It is also easy to pull up if you have too much of it, although it is hard to have too much. It brings a wonderful mix of blue, purple, and green shades to a border in spring and adds elegance to dry, sunny spots along pathway edges all through summer, where it can mingle well with plants from all styles, from traditional frothy alchemillas in early summer to bold rudbeckias later on.

**Plant type** Hardy annual

**Soil type** Dry, well-drained soil

**Aspect** Sun or semi-shade

**Height and spread** 60cm × 50cm (2ft × 1ft 8in)

**Season of interest** Spring and summer

## Clematis macropetala

*Clematis macropetala* is a special, stylish climbing plant for covering walls and doorways with beautiful blossom in spring. Its flowers have a peaceful, gently nodding nature, yet it is a hardy plant that can tolerate temperatures down to -20°C (-4°F). Leave the flowers intact on the plant once flowering has finished in early summer, and the most beautiful spidery seedheads will develop to clothe the plant with shimmering silvery strands that beautifully complement the finely fringed foliage.

**Plant type** Deciduous climber

**Soil type** Deep, well-drained soil

**Aspect** Sun or semi-shade

**Height and spread** 2.5m × 1.5m (8ft × 5ft)

**Season of interest** Spring to autumn

## Cleome hassleriana 'Helen Campbell'

Annuals grown from seed are not often thought of as backbone plants in the garden, but the airy, statuesque *Cleome hassleriana* 'Helen Campbell' will stand tall among substantial grasses such as *Miscanthus sinensis*, adding a light, floral touch with its unusual flower globes on sturdy, spiny (take care!) stems. It will continue looking pristine in the garden all summer. Sow indoors and plant in the middle of the border at the beginning of summer.

**Plant type** Half-hardy annual

**Soil type** Any well-drained soil

**Aspect** Full sun

**Height and spread** 1.2m × 60cm (4ft × 2ft)

**Season of interest** Summer

### *Coreopsis grandiflora* SunKiss

The modern cottage garden depends on a range of plants to start flowering in late summer to mingle with the ever-changing hues of the grasses and later flushes of flowers from roses and hollyhocks. *Coreopsis grandiflora* SunKiss does the job splendidly, sending up tight dark brown buds that burst into the sunniest rich yellow blooms with a maroon base, on thin stems that can weave themselves between the abundance of growth that fills the garden in summer. Its ruffled flowers will show until autumn, when they will blend tremendously well with brown and russet shades. A neat and compact plant, it will grow well among other plants in a container.

**Plant type** Herbaceous perennial

**Soil type** Any well-drained soil

**Aspect** Full sun

**Height and spread** 40cm × 40cm
(1ft 4in × 1ft 4in)

**Season of interest** Summer and
autumn

### *Cyclamen coum*

This dainty but tough perennial starts to flower in winter and is still in full bloom when the hedgerows and tree avenues are bursting into life in spring. *Cyclamen coum* grows best in a shady spot in soil that is not too rich and bulky. It will self-seed well in thin soil beneath trees if you have room, but it is also useful on a smaller scale. Try planting it in multiples around large evergreens in pots to add some old-fashioned charm in the cold months.

**Plant type** Perennial corm

**Soil type** Any well-drained soil

**Aspect** Shade

**Height and spread** 10cm × 20cm
(4in × 8in)

**Season of interest** Winter and
spring

## Echinacea purpurea 'Magnus'

Many echinaceas are available to gardeners today, all with varying degrees of hardiness, but 'Magnus' is among the easiest to grow. It is notable for its drooping petals, which sweep down on large flowers, and for its tall stature: it can tower up to a meter tall. *Echinacea purpurea* 'Magnus' won't get lost in the middle of a packed garden and is invaluable for a big sunny border that is in need of some height towards the back. It also grows well in containers placed in a sunny, sheltered position.

**Plant type** Herbaceous perennial

**Soil type** Any well-drained soil

**Aspect** Full sun

**Height and spread** 1m × 50cm
    (3ft 4in × 1ft 8in)

**Season of interest** Summer and
    autumn

## Erigeron karvinskianus

This pretty perennial has the ability to self-seed but is always forgiven because it has a way of enhancing the area where it grows and flowers. It is slow to get growing at the start of spring, but by the time summer arrives erigerons are gently trailing along paths or border edges and showing off dozens of daisy flowers, which have a neat pink flush on the underside of their petals and keep appearing into autumn. Full of old-fashioned charm, *Erigeron karvinskianus* is also capable of teaming up with grasses and evergreens to make something more contemporary looking.

**Plant type** Herbaceous perennial

**Soil type** Any well-drained soil

**Aspect** Sun or semi-shade

**Height and spread** 20cm × 1m
    (8in × 3ft 4in)

**Season of interest** Summer and
    autumn

### *Eryngium* ×*zabelii* 'Big Blue'

This variety of sea holly creates a big impact because of its large flowers displayed on a fairly short plant. The spiky flowerheads become more prominent as they age, darkening in colour as the summer progresses and proving useful for giving the garden definition in winter too. It needs a hot, dry sunny place in order to grow best, making it a good partner for erysimums, erigerons, and lavenders. Plant it against a dark backdrop so that the intricate shape of the flowers can be appreciated.

**Plant type** Herbaceous perennial

**Soil type** Any well-drained soil

**Aspect** Full sun

**Height and spread** 1m × 50cm
(3ft 4in × 1ft 8in)

**Season of interest** Summer, autumn, and winter

### *Erysimum* 'Bowles's Mauve'

When it comes to flower power, this neat perennial takes the first prize. Flowers appear for the first time in spring and new flowering stalks develop all through summer without a single break. The flowering season stretches into autumn and even winter if the plant is grown in a dry, sunny spot. *Erysimum* 'Bowles's Mauve' is a bushy perennial that needs trimming back in early spring to prevent it from going leggy. The perfect plant for providing reliable colour to a hot, dry location, this wallflower can bloom with tulips in spring and with eryngiums in late summer. Such a versatile plant!

**Plant type** Herbaceous perennial

**Soil type** Dry soil

**Aspect** Full sun

**Height and spread** 90cm × 45cm
(3ft × 1ft 6in)

**Season of interest** Spring and summer

## *Euphorbia amygdaloides* 'Purpurea'

Surely the ultimate plant for the modern cottage garden, *Euphorbia amygdaloides* 'Purpurea' effortlessly fits into both contemporary and traditional styles. Its warm blood-red new shoots blend well with spring bulbs, grasses, and early-flowering perennials such as saxifrage and pulmonaria, and the leaves are still a highlight as they age in summer and autumn and mingle with wispy grasses. The lime-green flowers give a vivid glow to late spring that will match the wow-factor of any tulip or daffodil.

**Plant type** Evergreen perennial

**Soil type** Any well-drained soil

**Aspect** Full sun

**Height and spread** 75cm × 75cm
(2ft 6in × 2ft 6in)

**Season of interest** Spring

## *Geranium* 'Patricia'

This hardy geranium is sterile, which means that rather than flowering and setting seed, *Geranium* 'Patricia' will just keep flowering and flowering through summer, clothing the garden with rich magenta for months. It can spread over two meters wide so it is suited to a large border. A fine partner for lime-greens and yellows, providing a sharp contrast, its loose, branching flower stems also make 'Patricia' suitable for growing among grasses, where the plants can blend together.

**Plant type** Herbaceous perennial

**Soil type** Any well-drained soil

**Aspect** Sun or semi-shade

**Height and spread** 1m × 2m
(3ft 4in × 6ft 7in)

**Season of interest** Summer and autumn

### *Geranium sylvaticum* 'Mayflower'

For a taste of summer in spring, this early-flowering hardy geranium proves irresistible. A plant with tall, upright stems rather than the more typical spreading growth of many hardy geraniums, *Geranium sylvaticum* 'Mayflower' can squeeze into gaps in the middle of a border where its pure blue flowers can mix with fresh new shoots of euphorbias and evergreen grasses. It will flower well in shade or sun. The leaves start to lose their lustre in summer, but they can be cut back to ground level and the plant will respond with fresh new foliage to provide a lush finish to the season.

**Plant type** Herbaceous perennial

**Soil type** Any damp soil

**Aspect** Sun or shade

**Height and spread** 70cm × 50cm
(2ft 4in × 1ft 8in)

**Season of interest** Spring

### *Geum* 'Totally Tangerine'

*Geum* 'Totally Tangerine' is sterile, so this beautiful perennial keeps flowering all summer long, providing warm colour to combine through the season with many more-transient flowers. Its tall, branching, flowering stems are good at blending in with other plants in a border and will provide a bold, complementary display of colour to purples from catmint, lavender, and *Erysimum* 'Bowles's Mauve', starting to flower at the end of spring to bridge the colour gap while we wait for summer.

**Plant type** Herbaceous perennial

**Soil type** Any well-drained soil

**Aspect** Full sun

**Height and spread** 1m × 50cm
(3ft 4in × 1ft 8in)

**Season of interest** Late spring
to autumn

## *Hedera helix* 'Ivalace'

While *Hedera helix* will climb as much as you let it to soften a wall or fence, 'Ivalace' is much shorter but very useful if you want to green up the space below a clematis or climbing rose with bare stems. It is self-clinging, with the glossiest of leaves. The leaves are a wonderfully dark green with unusual curled edges. Staying short, it can team up with perennial grasses to make an attractive, layered display of different greens.

**Plant type** Hardy shrub

**Soil type** Any soil

**Aspect** Shade or semi-shade

**Height and spread** 1m × 50cm
(3ft 4in × 1ft 8in)

**Season of interest** All year

## *Helenium autumnale* 'Helena Red Shades' (Helena Series)

When *Helenium autumnale* comes into bloom at the end of summer, it's an event akin to the first flowering bulbs of spring. The flowers of 'Helena Red Shades' add a warmth to the border that is unmistakably autumnal but also full of the vibrancy of summer. The tall, thin plant will grow among tall grasses, hollyhocks, and roses, where it will produce stems that branch at the top to hold many blooms, each of them long-lasting and indestructible. The flowers add form and texture to a border in winter if you leave them intact, making them a border highlight in their own right.

**Plant type** Herbaceous perennial

**Soil type** Any well-drained soil

**Aspect** Sun or semi-shade

**Height and spread** 70cm × 60cm
(2ft 4in × 2ft)

**Season of interest** Late summer and autumn

## *Heuchera* 'Sweet Tart' (Little Cutie Series)

The explosion of new varieties of *Heuchera* in gardens in recent decades has made this perennial something of a fashionable plant, but it is really a cottage garden classic that has been given a makeover by plant breeders. The zingy lime-green leaves of the short-growing variety 'Sweet Tart' add a spring-like freshness to a mixed border all through summer, and if planted in groups, the airy, luminous pink flowers ooze nostalgia and charm for a big impact. This is truly a plant to give you the best of both worlds, foliage and flowers. Vine weevil is a notorious pest of heucheras, but they are not as vulnerable if you grow them in the ground rather than containing their roots in a pot.

**Plant type** Herbaceous perennial

**Soil type** Any well-drained soil

**Aspect** Sun or semi-shade

**Height and spread** 15cm × 25cm (6in × 10in)

**Season of interest** Summer

## *Lamprocapnos spectabilis* 'Gold Heart'

If ever a plant could be described as ghostly, it is this spring-flowering perennial, long known as *Dicentra spectabilis*. It seems to pop up from nowhere in spring and rapidly transition to full bloom. Then by summer you will forget you ever saw it once the flowers wither and the stalks are cut off. Yet *Lamprocapnos spectabilis* 'Gold Heart' is worth growing for its undoubted cottage garden charm. The flower stalks bounce under the weight of the heart-shaped flowers, which add definition to a shady corner of the garden, while the fresh new gold foliage provides a sharp colour contrast.

**Plant type** Herbaceous perennial

**Soil type** Any damp soil

**Aspect** Shade or semi-shade

**Height and spread** 90cm × 90cm (3ft × 3ft)

**Season of interest** Spring

## *Lathyrus odoratus* Spencer Mixed

Perhaps the quintessential cottage garden climber, sweet peas are fantastic at adding height, scent, and constant colour to the garden. Spencer sweet peas are a tremendous form of sweet pea because of their large flowers and strong scent. Grow them up wigwams in a border and they can mix with tall herbaceous perennials and shrubs. Planted in early spring, they will be in flower at the start of summer and prompt deadheading will ensure a steady supply of the delicate, perfumed flowers into autumn. Water and feed them well through summer or they can run out of steam and develop mildew, and make sure you place them where you can easily access the plant to snip off the flowers.

**Plant type** Hardy annual climber

**Soil type** Moist, well-drained soil

**Aspect** Full sun

**Height and spread** 1.8m × 60cm (6ft × 2ft)

**Season of interest** Summer and autumn

## *Leptospermum scoparium*

*Leptospermum scoparium* is a pretty flowering shrub that blends well with perennials such as euphorbias in late spring and early summer. Known as the tea tree plant because of its needle-like leaves that release a scent when crushed, it forms a loose shape, merging well with its neighbours rather than being a blocky shrub. Its delicate, simple flowers are appealing to bees. Grow in dry soil in a warm, sheltered spot to help it survive the winter, or grow it in a pot and move it into a greenhouse for winter.

**Plant type** Borderline hardy shrub

**Soil type** Any well-drained soil, ideally acidic

**Aspect** Full sun and shelter

**Height and spread** 3m × 3m (10ft × 10ft)

**Season of interest** Spring and summer

## *Leucanthemum ×superbum* 'Goldfinch'

This daisy-flowered plant is a tough and reliable stalwart for freshening up the front of a border in summer. The flowers are durable, weather resistant, and around 10cm (4in) wide—those of 'Goldfinch' are a subtle buttery yellow fading to white—but the plant is short, which will save staking, which is necessary for taller forms. Shasta daisies flower in summer, but if you chop the plant back at the start of summer, it will start to flower in late summer and into early autumn. Slugs love these plants, so make sure you protect them.

**Plant type** Herbaceous perennial

**Soil type** Moist, well-drained soil

**Aspect** Sun or semi-shade

**Height and spread** 50cm × 60cm (1ft 8in × 2ft)

**Season of interest** Summer and autumn

## *Lonicera periclymenum* 'Serotina'

'Serotina' honeysuckle is a vigorous climber and the perfect candidate for sprawling over a wall, gate, or dead tree, where it will show off clouds of deliciously scented, spidery flowers in late summer and autumn. After flowering it holds clusters of shiny red fruits. Plant its roots in shade but give it a location where most of the stems will be in sun or semi-shade. Chop it back straight after flowering if it starts to outgrow its space.

**Plant type** Deciduous climber

**Soil type** Deep, well-drained soil

**Aspect** Sun or semi-shade

**Height and spread** 7m × 1.5m (21ft × 5ft)

**Season of interest** Spring to autumn

## Molinia caerulea subsp. caerulea 'Poul Petersen'

A fine grass that is most effective when planted in multiples, purple moor grass 'Poul Petersen' forms a neat and attractive fan of bright green leaves topped by graceful fountain-like flower stems that open a wonderful dark purple before lightening to a golden brown as they age. The leaves take on shades of gold and orange in autumn, creating a splendidly detailed display in the border.

**Plant type** Deciduous grass

**Soil type** Moist, well-drained soil

**Aspect** Sun or semi-shade

**Height and spread** 80cm × 60cm
(2ft 8in × 2ft)

**Season of interest** Summer and
autumn

## Nepeta grandiflora 'Summer Magic'

Catmint is a majestic plant for gracing a border edge, with sprays of mauve flowers perfectly accompanied by soft, grey-green leaves. *Nepeta grandiflora* 'Summer Magic' is more upright and not as sprawling as some of the bigger varieties of catmint, and it makes a neat, drought-resistant plant for a container. It is also a fine plant to include underneath a rose or alongside a euphorbia. If you have a problem with cats rolling in it— they love the scent of the leaves—then try growing it in a hanging basket.

**Plant type** Herbaceous perennial

**Soil type** Any well-drained soil

**Aspect** Full sun

**Height and spread** 40cm × 40cm
(1ft 4in × 1ft 4in)

**Season of interest** Summer

## *Panicum virgatum*

If you want a manageable plant that looks good for most of the year, this slender grass is a fine choice and adds some simple but effective architecture to a border. *Panicum virgatum* is especially effective at breaking up a barren landscape in winter and highlighting darker perennials in the foreground, and it will cope well with exposure to strong winds. During spring and summer it has attractive blue-green foliage, with pink-tinged flowers in autumn.

**Plant type** Deciduous grass

**Soil type** Any well-drained soil

**Aspect** Sun or shade

**Height and spread** 1.8m × 90cm
  (6ft × 3ft)

**Season of interest** All year

## *Rosa* 'Felicia'

If you are put off by the idea of roses because you think of the tall, large-flowered, leggy plants in municipal parks, try this one. 'Felicia' is a bushy plant, growing as wide as it is tall and producing small, intricate, but understated flowers that are good enough for a suit buttonhole when in bud. The buds are red before revealing flowers in shell pink. This is an unobtrusive plant that is a team player rather than a glory seeker, growing well with alchemillas and short grasses.

**Plant type** Hardy shrub

**Soil type** Any moisture-retentive soil

**Aspect** Sun or semi-shade

**Height and spread** 1.2m × 1.2m
  (4ft × 4ft)

**Season of interest** Summer and
  early autumn

## *Rosa* 'Princess Anne'

'Princess Anne' is among the most compact of English roses, short in stature and with small but pretty, rounded, very glossy, healthy leaves. Despite the plant's small stature, the flowers are full size, red in bud before opening to the deepest mauve, then ageing beautifully to a softer pink. The flowers have a fruity fragrance, too, and a tantalizing streak of yellow at the base of the petals. It is often recommended for containers because of its size, but it also makes for a high-impact plant for edging a border and will provide at least three flushes of flowers a year in a small space.

**Plant type** Hardy shrub

**Soil type** Any moisture-retentive soil

**Aspect** Sun or semi-shade

**Height and spread** 1.2m × 90cm (4ft × 3ft)

**Season of interest** Summer and early autumn

## *Rosa* 'The Pilgrim'

'The Pilgrim' rose has the most perfectly formed flowers, with a rich lemon-yellow colouring in the centre that fades gently to the edge of the flower. This is a very free-flowering rose that produces blooms all the way along the plant to clothe garden boundaries in flowers, and it can also be grown as a large shrub if you chop it back hard each spring. The flowers have a fresh scent and form rain-resistant rosettes when fully out.

**Plant type** Hardy shrub

**Soil type** Any moisture-retentive soil

**Aspect** Sun or semi-shade

**Height and spread** 4m × 1.2m (13ft × 4ft)

**Season of interest** Summer and autumn

## *Rudbeckia fulgida* var. *sullivantii* 'Goldsturm'

A true classic in many new perennial gardens, the bright and cheerful 'Goldsturm' rudbeckia is popular for a good reason. Its stems are sturdy and strong and the flowers durable, consistent in colour, and neat in form as a pleasing-looking dome of colour towards the end of summer. Their attractive shape looks good in the depths of winter too. Partial to damp, quite heavy soil, they make surprisingly good partners for roses, which allows you effortlessly to create wonderfully bright and colourful pockets in a border. Although they look similar to echinaceas, rudbeckias are not as tolerant of drought conditions.

**Plant type** Herbaceous perennial

**Soil type** Any moisture-retentive soil

**Aspect** Sun or semi-shade

**Height and spread** 60cm × 60cm (2ft × 2ft)

**Season of interest** Late summer and autumn

## *Salvia* 'Hot Lips'

This bushy sub-shrub is only hardy down to around -10°C (14°F) but is still worth growing if winters are colder and you have to treat it as an annual plant. *Salvia* 'Hot Lips' starts flowering in summer and continues through until the first frost. It is a versatile plant for a mixed border, with its airy flowers borne on thin stems mixing well with other plants but never becoming obtrusive. Also a neat grower, it provides a fine platform for taller perennials to grow around.

**Plant type** Borderline hardy sub-shrub

**Soil type** Any well-drained soil

**Aspect** Full sun

**Height and spread** 1m × 1m (3ft 4in × 3ft 4in)

**Season of interest** Summer to late autumn

## *Saxifraga* 'Peter Pan'

The edges of pots and borders can look gappy and bare in spring, which is where this pretty saxifrage becomes a useful plant. It forms a low hummock of tiny evergreen leaves, but these will be unnoticed in spring and early summer because 'Peter Pan' will be smothered in hot pink flowers that age gracefully to white, creating a wonderful colour contrast between old and new blossoms. Pair it with the new red shoots of *Euphorbia amygdaloides* 'Purpurea' for a delightfully rich colour combo in a spring container.

**Plant type** Evergreen perennial

**Soil type** Any well-drained soil

**Aspect** Full sun

**Height and spread** 10cm × 50cm (4in × 1ft 8in)

**Season of interest** Spring

## *Sedum* 'Matrona'

An ideal perennial for displaying perfectly preserved seedheads in the garden in winter, *Sedum* (or *Hylotelephium*) 'Matrona' is a hard-working plant. Its fleshy leaves have an intriguing purple tinge to them and the stems are an intense maroon red. The summer flowers are palest pink, providing a wonderful contrast with the foliage below, with one offsetting the other. Stout and compact, the plant appears unmoved by the end of winter, with the perfectly preserved old stems protecting the new shoots at the base, a glorious reminder of the growing season to come and of the one that has passed.

**Plant type** Hardy perennial

**Soil type** Any well-drained soil

**Aspect** Full sun

**Height and spread** 75cm × 60cm (2ft 6in × 2ft)

**Season of interest** Summer to winter

## Selinum wallichianum

*Selinum wallichianum* will add an invaluable splash of spring finery to the garden at the end of summer and into autumn. The umbel flowers bring a fresh, frothy finesse to the border at a time when colours can start to dull, and the seedheads will add character to the garden in winter too. It is the perfect partner for tall grasses and shrub roses, helping bridge the gap between traditional and contemporary styles of planting. Remember to stake this plant in spring to keep it stocky.

**Plant type** Herbaceous perennial

**Soil type** Damp but well-drained soil

**Aspect** Sun or semi-shade

**Height and spread** 1.5m × 50cm
(5ft × 1ft 8in)

**Season of interest** Summer,
autumn, and winter

## Sesleria autumnalis

*Sesleria autumnalis* creates neat, low mounds of grass that gracefully fan out rather than standing tall, making it useful for hiding the bases of taller shrubs and perennials. The leaves are an intriguing yellow-green and can stay intact all year in a mild winter. In summer it sends out attractive horizontal flower stalks that are like slim, miniature pampas grass flowers in the shape of exploding fireworks (on the right in the photo).

**Plant type** Semi-evergreen grass

**Soil type** Any well-drained soil

**Aspect** Sun or semi-shade

**Height and spread** 50cm × 30cm
(1ft 8in × 1ft)

**Season of interest** Winter and
spring

## *Spiraea japonica* 'Goldflame'

*Spiraea japonica* 'Goldflame' is a shrub with many facets, showing the most glorious new shoots—a heady mix of bronze and red—as the leaves emerge from bare stems in spring. The leaves age to lime-green, then golden yellow, and the flowerheads holds clusters of tiny hot pink flowers that stand out handsomely among the bright summer leaves. It forms a neat mound for a container or the front of a border, and the flowers will attract butterflies.

**Plant type** Hardy deciduous shrub

**Soil type** Any well-drained soil

**Aspect** Full sun

**Height and spread** 75cm × 75cm
(2ft 6in × 2ft 6in)

**Season of interest** Spring to
late summer

## *Sporobolus heterolepis*

*Sporobolus heterolepis* (on the right in the photo) is a favourite plant of the great Piet Oudolf, and in 2016 he named the slightly taller variety 'Weinheim' as his top new plant of the previous twenty years, praising its ability to look good all through the year. Even in the depths of winter the graceful shape of *Sporobolus heterolepis* is unmistakeable; in summer its leaves stay low to show off the upright sprays of golden brown flowers, providing an effective way to create a dense, full border. The flowers have a distinctive scent similar to that of coriander.

**Plant type** Deciduous grass

**Soil type** Any soil except waterlogged

**Aspect** Full sun

**Height and spread** 90cm × 60cm
(3ft × 2ft)

**Season of interest** All year

## Stipa gigantea

With this grass the clue is in the species name. *Stipa* (or *Nassella*) *gigantea* does get very tall, but it has a gracefulness about it that means it isn't a brute at full height. Its arching flower stems give the plant a fountain-like form in high summer as they drip with the golden flowerheads that look like oats (seedheads are at the back in the photo). Although traditionally planted at the back of a border, it can also work well in the middle of large spaces, making a fine focal point. It is hardy to around -10°C (14°F).

**Plant type** Borderline hardy
   semi-evergreen grass

**Soil type** Any well-drained soil

**Aspect** Full sun

**Height and spread** 2.5m × 90cm
   (8ft 4in × 3ft)

**Season of interest** Summer

## Stipa tenuissima

This wispy grass—which is sometimes evergreen and sometimes deciduous—is a light and elegant plant to grow if you don't have the scale of garden for the more vigorous grasses that can tower above the tallest person you know. *Stipa* (or *Nassella*) *tenuissima* (on the right in the photo) is superb for knitting together the edge of a border where it moves gracefully in the wind, adding a soft frothiness to the garden. Invaluable for softening plantings but never obtrusive, this is a plant that it is difficult to have too much of.

**Plant type** Evergreen grass

**Soil type** Any well-drained soil

**Aspect** Sun or semi-shade

**Height and spread** 60cm × 50cm
   (2ft × 1ft 8in)

**Season of interest** All year,
   flowers in summer

# Resources

Hamilton, Geoff. *Geoff Hamilton's Cottage Gardens*. London: BBC Books, 1995.

Lord, Tony, Andrew Lawson, and the Royal Horticultural Society (Great Britain). *RHS Encyclopedia of Planting Combinations*. New edition. London: Mitchell Beazley, 2012.

National Garden Scheme. www.ngs.org.uk. This initiative allows private gardeners to open their garden gates in return for an admission fee given to charity. If you are garden-visiting in the UK, seeing those in the National Garden Scheme is a great way to pick up ideas and inspiration for your own garden while helping good causes.

Oudolf, Piet, and Henk Gerritsen. *Planting the Natural Garden*. Revised edition. Portland, OR: Timber Press, 2019.

Oudolf, Piet, and Noel Kingsbury. *Planting: A New Perspective*. Portland, OR: Timber Press, 2013.

Péreire, Anita. *Gardens for the 21st Century*. London: Aurum Press, 1999.

Robinson, William. *The Wild Garden*. London: John Murray, 1894.

# Acknowledgements

Thanks to all those at Timber Press who have made this book possible and given me the opportunity, especially Becky O'Malley, who first suggested that I should consider pitching book ideas. To Eve Goodman, for sharing her experience and for masterfully editing the manuscript in such a positive and forensic way. Big thanks also to Tom Fischer, for believing in the idea and helping it get the green light. Additional thanks to Andrew Beckman, Sarah Milhollin, and Alex Fus at Timber, for their help in explaining and guiding me through the publishing process. Many thanks to Sarah Crumb and the design team for their wonderful work in bringing these words and pictures to life.

Many people have encouraged and supported me over the years that I have written about gardening. Geoff Stebbings for sharing his unbelievable gardening knowledge so generously with me and for helping me to never take myself too seriously. And thanks Geoff, along with Neil Pope and Clare Foggett, for believing that it was worth giving a very under-qualified twenty-something a chance in the world of magazine writing. Thanks also to Clare for encouraging me over the years, giving me so many amazing writing opportunities, introducing me to so many people, and for helping me understand just how much can be achieved in a short space of time!

Thank you to everyone who gave so generously of their time, talents, resources, and gardens for this book.

To Piet Oudolf for taking the time to talk to me about his approach to planting a garden. To Mark Straver and Robin Wallis at Hortus Loci, in Hampshire, UK, for allowing me to tour the nursery and discover new, expertly grown plants, many of which are featured in the book.

To Michael Marriott and David Austin Roses in Wolverhampton, UK, for advising on varieties that would grow well in my garden and supplying plants and to Nicola Bethell at Davis Austin Roses for her help with images. Both Hortus Loci and David Austin Roses UK and US can also be found online.

To Jenny Bowden, Robert Marshall, and Richard Handscombe for allowing their gardens to be photographed. To Jo Artherton and Jonathan Pearce at Pensthorpe Natural Park, Celine Leslie at Gravetye Manor, Grant Mantle at the Trentham Estate, Stephen and Kim Rogers at Dove Cottage Nursery, Mike Werkmeister at East Lambrook Manor Gardens, Charlotte Kirton and Paul Smith at Scampston Walled Garden, and Louise Scott and Mark Jackson at Newby Hall. Thanks, Mark, for your generosity of time and expertise at Newby Hall during such a hot and dry summer.

Also thanks to Jess Cook at Silver Ball PR, Sarah Sandys-Renton at BBC Gardeners' World Live, and Camilla Harrison at Harrogate Flower Show.

To Neil Hepworth for the amazing pictures, the travelling, the ideas, the car journeys, for putting up with blazing sun in July during one of the hottest UK summers on record and pouring rain in the middle of winter, and for being flexible, creative, and supportive. This book wouldn't have happened without you.

And thanks to my family for loving, supporting, and encouraging. Thanks, Mum and Dad, for letting me loose on your garden when I was just starting out and for giving me the opportunity to discover the joys of an outdoor life from a young age. Thanks to my amazing wife for putting up with the late nights in front of the laptop, the absent summer days, and the times when chasing deadlines meant that other things were neglected. You and our son, Malachi, bring more joy than you will ever know, and I am blessed beyond words to have you both in my life.

And last but most importantly, thank you, God, my maker, sustainer, and eternal hope.

# Photography Credits

**All photographs are by Neil Hepworth except for the following:**

Alamy/Tim Gainey: page 75 (left)

David Austin Roses / Howard Rice: pages 11, 114 (middle), 145, 147, 184 (fourth from left)

Getty / Neil Holmes: page 204 (right)

Gravetye Manor: pages 18, 21

Greg Loades: pages 82 (left), 96 (top left), 100 (right)

Pensthorpe Natural Park / Mike Powles: page 33 (top)

Shutterstock / Alybaba: page 177

Shutterstock / Anna Gratys: page 185 (left)

Shutterstock / Del Boy: page 132

Shutterstock / Ian Driscoll: page 208 (right)

Shutterstock / LFRobanedo: page 146

Shutterstock / Lianem: page 192 (right)

Shutterstock / Lmladris: page 175

Shutterstock / Martien Van Gaalen: page 185 (right)

Shutterstock / Mizy: pages 165 (top), 176

Shutterstock / Simona Pavan: pages 136, 165 (bottom)

Shutterstock / Vladimir Salman: page 172

Trentham Gardens / Joe Wainwright: pages 36, 37

**Additional Garden Credits:**

Churt Lea Cottage, page 66

Dove Cottage Nursery, page 222

Newby Hall, pages 74, 78, 80 (bottom), 81, 140, 156, 161 (top)

Pensthorpe Natural Park, pages 75 (right), 173, 174, 184 (second from left)

Scampston Walled Garden, pages 32, 49, 71, 80 (top), 114 (right), 158, 162, 163, 205

# Index

**Greg Loades** is editor of *The Alpine Gardener*, quarterly journal of the Alpine Garden Society, and writes frequently about gardens and gardening for magazines such as *Kew*, *LandScape*, and *Garden News*. His writing has also appeared in many popular publications, including *BBC Gardeners' World* magazine, where he was gardening editor, and the luxury garden publication *The English Garden*, where he was deputy editor. He served his apprenticeship in the rose industry in the UK. Today Greg lives in Hull with his wife and son and has a small backyard terraced house garden packed with perennials, grasses, and, of course, roses! Follow his gardening life on Instagram: @hull_urban_gardener.

**Neil Hepworth** is a freelance photographer with over twenty years' experience whose clients include the Royal Horticultural Society. Neil covers flower shows for the RHS and photographs around forty gardens a year for other clients.